Granicus 334 BC

Alexander's first Persian victory

Campaign • 182

Granicus 334 BC

Alexander's first Persian victory

Michael Thompson · Illustrated by Richard Hook

First published in Great Britain in 2007 by Osprey Publishing,
Midland House, West Way, Botley, Oxford OX2 9LP, United Kingdom.
443 Park Avenue South, New York, NY 10016, USA
Email: info@ospreypublishing.com

A CIP catalogue record for this book is available from the British Library.

ISBN 978 1 84603 099 4

The author, Michael Thompson, has asserted his right under the Copyright,
Designs and Patents Act, 1988, to be identified as the Author of this Work.

Page layouts by The Black Spot
Typeset in Helvetica and ITC New Baskerville
Index: Glyn Sutcliffe
Maps by The Map Studio
3d bird's-eye views by The Black Spot
Battlescene artwork by Richard Hook
Originated by PPS Grasmere Ltd, Leeds, UK
Printed and bound in China through Worldprint Ltd

07 08 09 10 11   10 9 8 7 6 5 4 3 2 1

For a catalogue of all books published by Osprey please contact:
Osprey Direct UK, PO Box 140, Wellingborough,
Northants, NN8 2FA, UK
Email: info@ospreydirect.co.uk

North America
Osprey Direct, c/o Random House Distribution Center, 400 Hahn Road,
Westminster, MD 21157
Email: info@ospreydirect.com

www.ospreypublishing.com

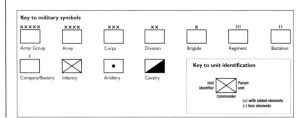

CONTENTS

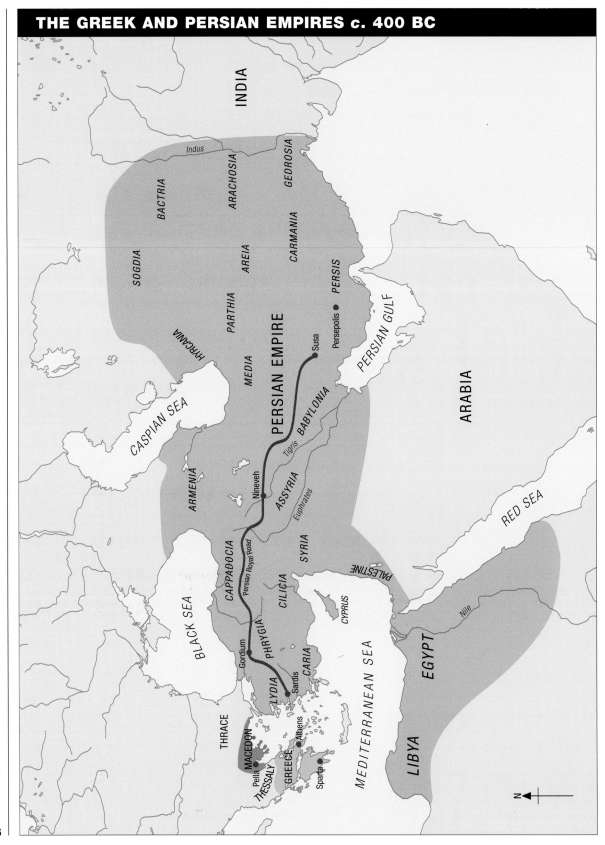

INDIA

Indus

ARACHOSIA

GEDROSIA

BACTRIA

CARMANIA

SOGDIA

AREIA

PERSIS

Persepolis

PERSIAN GULF

PARTHIA

PERSIAN EMPIRE

HYRCANIA

MEDIA

Susa

BABYLONIA

ARABIA

CASPIAN SEA

Tigris

ARMENIA

Nineveh

ASSYRIA

Euphrates

RED SEA

CAPPADOCIA

Persian Royal Road

SYRIA

PALESTINE

BLACK SEA

CILICIA

Nile

Gordium

PHRYGIA

CYPRUS

LYDIA

Sardis

CARIA

EGYPT

THRACE

MEDITERRANEAN SEA

MACEDON

Athens

LIBYA

Pella

GREECE

Sparta

THESSALY

N

INTRODUCTION

THE GRAECO-PERSIAN WARS

I n 490 BC, Darius I, the Great King of Persia, launched a military expedition against Greece. Five years earlier, he had already quelled a revolt of the Ionian Greek city-states of western Anatolia (modern Turkey) and now sought revenge against those mainland Greek cities that had supported them. An invasion force was landed on the plain of Marathon roughly 20 miles north of Athens, where it was met and defeated by a combined force of Athenian and Plataean hoplites.

Undeterred by this setback, Darius' successor, Xerxes, led another, larger expedition against Greece and the Athenians in particular. Crossing the Hellespont into Europe in 480 BC, he accepted Macedon's surrender and marched south through Thessaly towards central Greece and Attica. A contingent of 300 Spartans blocking the pass at Thermopylae was eventually overcome, leaving open the road to Athens and the Peloponnese. Unable to confront the massive Persian army on land, the Athenians abandoned their city and looked to their powerful

A relief from Persepolis showing Darius I seated, with Xerxes I standing behind him. (Werner Forman Archive/Archaeological Museum, Teheran)

navy to face the Persians. Athens itself was duly sacked and burned but the Persian navy suffered a heavy defeat off the neighbouring island of Salamis. Xerxes himself returned to Sardis while a considerable force under Mardonius was wintered in Thessaly, in northern Greece, intending to resume the campaign the following year. Having persuaded the Spartans to confront the Persians, the Greeks engaged and defeated the Persian army at Plataea in Boeotia in 479 BC. In the same year, the Persian navy was defeated again at Mycale, ending Persian military adventures in Greece.

Classical Greece

Although the kings of Persia would not return to Greece with a military force, they constantly meddled in her internal affairs through diplomatic and other means. Financial support and the prospect of military intervention in favour of one city-state (in Greek, *polis*, pl. *poleis*) or another in the constant internecine struggles was a destabilizing factor in Greek internal relations throughout the first half of the 5th century BC. By 449 BC, however, Persia disavowed any formal ambition of conquering Greece with the so-called Peace of Callias agreed with Athens. The détente

ensured the hegemony of Athens over the Delian league and her interests in the Aegean basin in return for similar respect for the Persian sphere of influence in western Asia, Palestine and Egypt.

This state of affairs continued for the next 30 years until the lure of intervention in the Peloponnesian War between Sparta and her allies and Athens and the Delian league proved too difficult for the Persians to resist. At the end of a 30-year struggle with her greatest rival, in 401 BC, Athens eventually succumbed to Sparta and sued for peace. Sparta's victory and leadership of the Greek world was not long-lived, however, as Thebes in Boeotia grew in strength and contested for hegemony while Athens herself, spared the annihilation asked for by Corinth and others at the end of the Peloponnesian War, rose again to considerable power and influence with the Second Athenian confederation. During these power struggles in Greece in the first half of the 4th century BC, Persia maintained her interest in a divided Greece by playing the city-states against each other. The allure of Persian gold often proved a temptation too great amongst the warring city-states in their struggles for hegemony.

These internal divisions did not go unnoticed by some in Greece, such as the rhetorician Isocrates, who lamented the exhausting and fruitless feuding amongst Greeks. This, he thought, could best be overcome by their uniting in a crusade of retribution against Persia for the sacrilegious crimes which were committed against Greece a century earlier. Although the theory of pan-Hellenism promulgated in the rhetorical flourishes of Isocrates did not always match the *realpolitik* of conflicts between the Greek *poleis*–as noted, Sparta, which was not alone, had accepted Persian support both during and after the Peloponnesian wars and Macedon, perhaps out of necessity, had gone over to the

The rhetorician Isocrates was the most vocal proponent of Hellenic unity in order to avenge the Persian attacks on Greece at the beginning of the 5th century BC. He wrote a series of pamphlets from 380 to 346 BC urging various Greek leaders to unite Greece in an expedition against Persia.

This reconstruction of the head of Alexander's father, Philip II, was made on the basis of skeletal remains discovered in 1977 in the Macedonian royal tombs at Vergina. The damage to Philip's left eye occurred at the siege of Methone in 354 BC. (The University of Manchester)

Persians during the invasions of the early 5th century BC–the ideal remained a powerful intellectual construct (Austin, 204). A commitment to 'freedom' (*eleutheria*), what we might today call a right to self-determination, was deeply valued throughout Greek society, despite the apparently contradictory fact that city-states were not averse to sacrificing the freedom of fellow Greeks if it was in the interests of their own *polis*. This was particularly the case when Greek city-states on the margins of the Persian Empire, as in western Anatolia, found their independence under threat. These *poleis* occasionally found themselves sold out by fellow Greeks on the mainland in order to curry favour with the Persians, as happened with the so-called King's Peace of 386 BC when Sparta accepted Persian dominion over the cities of western Asia Minor in return for their support of Spartan hegemony in Greece. Despite this apparent inconsistency, 'liberation' of Greeks from the yoke of Persian rule was a concept and project often lauded. If not exactly wrath, Sparta did incur some shame from fellow Greeks in what could be portrayed as their treacherous dealings with the old enemy Persia.

Nevertheless, by the middle of the 4th century BC, after a half-century of internal struggles, no one city-state in Greece was in a position to undertake such leadership nor, it seems, did any have the will. A new power to the north of the heartland of Greece, however, was soon to be in such a position and under the leadership of its king, Philip II, Macedon was gradually to take up the call.

The Rise of Macedon

The origins of the Macedonian state in antiquity are obscure, as they were to the classical Greeks who generally regarded the inhabitants as semi-barbarous and residing on the periphery of the civilized world. According to tradition, the Argead line of kings was founded in the 8th century BC but little is heard of them until Herodotus related the role of Alexander I during the Persian invasions. In that instance, the Macedonians somewhat reluctantly co-operated with the Persians but were quick to reassert their independence after the Persian withdrawal. The exact nature of formal Macedonian kingship is also unclear, but accession to the throne was often subject to internal and foreign intrigue, including assassination, with no less than 13 monarchs ruling from Alexander I to Philip II; a period of less than 100 years. By 359 BC Philip II had become king of the Macedonians and was to usher in their ascent to the world stage. A contemporary historian, Theopompus of Chios, claimed that 'Europe had never before produced such a man as Philip' (F. Jacoby, *Die Fragmente der griechischen Historiker* 115 [Theopompus] Fragment 27) and his elevation of the previously derided Macedon to regional dominance was an impressive and startling achievement.

The son of Amyntas III, Philip II of Macedon had spent time in Thebes as a noble hostage before he was appointed regent in his early twenties to an infant nephew. Philip soon removed this obstacle to his kingship and assumed the crown in 359 BC. He quickly began to reorganize the Macedonian army, taking into consideration the advances in warfare developed by the Thebans. In particular, he would have noted the tactical innovations of the two great Theban military commanders, Epaminondas and Pelopidas. By lengthening the leftmost columns of the traditional hoplite (heavy infantry) battle line and co-ordinating cavalry to attack the flanks of the enemy, Epaminondas was able to lead the Boeotians to victory over Sparta and her Peloponnesian allies in decisive battles at Leuctra (371 BC) and 'second' Mantinea (362 BC), effectively ending Spartan supremacy in Greece. These innovations highlighted the changing nature of warfare in the 4th century BC. No longer would the traditional clash of heavy armed classical hoplites alone prove decisive on the battlefield. Rethinking the use and nature of heavy infantry, the place and role of light armed auxiliaries and, most importantly, the integration of cavalry into the battlefield were crucial lessons to be learned.

Philip in the north

Philip began his reign by consolidating the border regions to the north-west of the Macedonian homeland which, at that time, was bounded by the mountainous regions of Epirus, Illyria, and Paeonia to the west and north; the Strymon river and Thrace to the east; and the Greek state of Thessaly to the south. Historically, these upland border regions, with their tough, warlike hill tribes, had proved a source of almost constant difficulty to the Macedonian state. In fact, Philip's usurpation of the throne followed his brother, Perdiccas III's, disastrous defeat at the hands of the Illyrians in 360 BC. The historian Diodorus stated (16.2.4-5) that over 4,000 Macedonians had been killed in the battle. After a thorough reorganization and retraining of the army, it was towards this precarious area that Philip turned his attentions in the summer of 358 BC. Defeating the Illyrian king, Bardylis, with an intriguing use of outflanking cavalry, Philip proceeded to further consolidate relations on his western borders through marriage to the daughter of the king of the Molossians, the most significant of the tribes in the highlands of Epirus. With this wife, Olympias, he would father his second son, Alexander III (i.e. 'the Great') in 356 BC.

With the situation in the north and west stabilized, Philip turned east where vigilance of the formidable tribes of Thrace was always required. In addition, the wealthy Greek *poleis* in and around the Chalcidice drew his interest. Amphipolis, astride the Strymon river on the route to the Hellespont, was an Athenian colony settled in 437 BC. Moreover, its hinterland was rich in timber and bordered Mt Pangaion, a prodigious source of gold and silver. In 357 BC, Philip besieged the city, which fell within weeks, much to the consternation of the Athenians who had regarded it as their satellite. Other Greek *poleis* in the Chalcidice and around the Thermaic Gulf would fall to Philip in successive campaigns, either through intrigue or force of arms: Potidea (356 BC); Pydna (356 BC); Crenides (355 BC); Methone (354 BC); and ultimately, Olynthus (348 BC).

Up to this point Philip had contented himself with securing the Balkan frontiers and picking off those Greek *poleis* in the northern

The 'Lion of Chaeronea' is thought to mark the spot where the Thebans were destroyed by the Macedonian army at the battle of Chaeronea in 338 BC. (Jona Lendering, www.livius.org)

Aegean which Athens, or any other Greek city-state of the south, was unable or unwilling to support. Although his military exploits were no doubt impressive, there does not seem to have been any explicit imperial impulse to his actions. Certainly, the Macedonian state was increasing in wealth and power, but Philip was usually satisfied to make defensive alliances with potentially quarrelsome neighbours or simply buy them off with bribes. Of course, force and the threat of force was sufficient to achieve these limited aims, but Philip, as Diodorus notes (16.95.1–4) was a very shrewd manipulator of diplomatic processes, which for the Macedonian royal line often meant political alliances through marriage. This aspect of Philip's foreign policy should not be overlooked nor should the Macedonians' acceptance of polygamy in the service of political aims. One ancient author commented that 'Philip always married a new wife with each new war he undertook' (Satyrus quoted in Athenaeus *Deipnosophists* 13.557c–e). Although that claim is exaggerated, marriage to women from Illyria, Elymiotis, Molossia, Thrace, and Pherae and Larissa in Thessaly helped Philip secure vital border regions without recourse to constant, resource-draining military adventures.

Philip in the south
In the mid 350s BC Athens was embroiled in the 'Social War' which saw her expending energy to reassert control over rebellious allies while Philip, under the guise of supporting one side in a conflict between *poleis* on the island Euboea, seized a subtle opportunity to meddle in the affairs of southern mainland Greece. He was fully able to insinuate himself as a player in mainland Greece during the (third) 'Sacred War' of 356–346 BC. This decade-long conflict would further weaken an already war-weary Greece.

In 356 BC a dispute arose over pressure the Phocians were exerting on the sacred priestesses at Delphi. Fearing that the more powerful Thebes would remove their influence at Delphi, the Phocians seized the sanctuary and extorted money from the Delphians to raise a large mercenary army. Later they were to plunder the sacred treasuries and melt down bronze and iron from the temple statues to support their war

The eastern façade of the Parthenon on the Acropolis of Athens. Alexander dedicated 300 captured panoplies to Athena after his victory at the Granicus. Some of the armour may have been placed on the architrave above the columns. (Jona Lendering, www.livius.org)

The Athenian orator Demosthenes was a vociferous opponent of Philip II. In a series of speeches known as the *Philippics* he attempted to rouse Athenian opposition to Philip.

effort. Enraged at this sacrilege, Thebes enlisted their Boeotian allies, the Locrians, and the Thessalians amongst others, against Phocis who in turn garnered the support of Athens, Sparta and some of Sparta's Peloponnesian allies. While some desultory and indecisive engagements occurred between the two sides over the next three years, Philip completed his stranglehold on the cities of the Thermaic Gulf by sacking Methone and capturing Pagasae.

However, Philip was able to exert a more pointed influence in these southern affairs when he was invited by the Thessalian League to bring the rebellious city of Pherae back into the fold. After an initial success against the Phocians who had come to support Pherae, Philip was seriously defeated in two battles by the full Phocian army led by Onomarchus. Undeterred by these setbacks, Philip rallied the Macedonian army and, with the support of the Thessalian cavalry, crushed the Phocian and allied army at the battle of Crocus Field in 352 BC, massacring the 'temple-robbers' and crucifying their leader Onomarchus. Buoyed by this success, Philip probed farther south into central Greece. Beginning to realize the danger, Athens blocked the pass at Thermopylae, whereupon Philip retired.

Nevertheless, Philip had achieved a number of goals. His service to Thessaly saw him appointed *tagus*, or leader, of the League, which was renowned for its rich horse-rearing plains and concomitant expert cavalry. Furthermore, when Phocis ultimately surrendered in 346 BC, their two votes on the Amphictionic Council, which administered the sacred site of Delphi, were given to Philip who championed himself as protector of the sanctuary and avenger of the impious who had defiled it. On the other hand, southern Greece, riven by this indecisive and costly warfare was further weakened.

The battle of Chaeronea

Following his gains in the south at the end of the Sacred War, Philip decided not to exacerbate the hostility emanating from an agitated Athens, where the orator Demosthenes fulminated against the Macedonian king in a series of speeches known as the *Philippics*. In 346 BC an uneasy peace was made with Athens, and Philip returned once again to affairs in the north where he overcame Thracian opposition and extended his power to the Hellespont and the Propontis (Sea of Marmara). By this time it was becoming increasingly evident to the *poleis* and states of Greece that the most dangerous and volatile threat to their independence was from Macedon. In 348 BC the prosperous city of Olynthus pleaded for Athenian help when besieged by Philip. Only a pittance was forthcoming, and when the city duly fell a wrathful Philip razed it to the ground and sold off the population as slaves. Perinthus and Byzantium were besieged in 341 BC and when Philip seized Athenian grain ships in the Hellespont alarm bells were sounded in Athens. Grain shipments from the Black Sea were the life-blood of Athenian sustenance and these incursions could not be tolerated. Thebes, marginalized from their fellow Boeotians by the machinations of Philip, also realized the potential dangers of a Macedon perched on their very doorstep. They received overtures from the Persian Empire, which, wary of Philip's meddling near north-west Anatolia, reverted to its previous diplomatic strategy in Greece and sought to aid other Greeks against the latest emerging power.

This image of the ancient historian Plutarch comes from a 1559 French translation of his works. Plutarch's *Life of Alexander* is one of the main sources of information on the battle of the Granicus along with Diodorus Siculus and Arrian, two other ancient historians.

By 338 BC events had come to a head. Although Philip had often tried to placate Athenian and Greek unease over his activities, it was apparent that the time for a confrontation with Thebes and Athens could no longer be avoided. Philip, now accompanied by his 18-year-old son, Alexander, led his army south into Phocis and seized the city of Elateia on the Boeotian border which bypassed the strategic pass at Thermopylae. The route to Thebes and Athens now lay open. A frantic Athenian embassy led by Demosthenes was sent to their old enemy, Thebes, seeking an alliance against Macedon. An alliance having been agreed, the full Athenian army joined the Thebans and loyal Boeotian allies at the town of Chaeronea. In early August, Philip at the head of the full Macedonian army of 30,000 infantry and roughly 2,000 cavalry met them on the valley plain outside the little town.

Philip took command of the Macedonian right wing while Alexander was positioned on the left with the other Macedonian generals. It may have been the case that Alexander commanded the cavalry which had been lined up against the Theban Sacred Band on the Greek far right, but cavalry are not explicitly mentioned in the sources (Rahe (1981), Gaebel, 155–7). The Sacred Band, an elite infantry unit of 150 paired lovers, was hitherto the most effective fighting force in the Greek world and occupied the traditional prestige position on the right of the battle line. An ancient military writer remarks that Philip withdrew his phalanx on the left in order to lure the Athenians opposite him into a rash charge (Polyaenus *Stratagems of War* 4.2.2). In this way he hoped to open a gap in the Greek line which Alexander could exploit with his cavalry. As the Macedonian line advanced obliquely, pivoting on a point near Philip which also allowed his feigned retreat, the Athenians moved forwards stretching the centre in their effort to maintain the integrity of the Greek

front. A gap was opened into which Alexander attacked, isolating the Sacred Band which he wheeled upon and completely destroyed. Philip in turn attacked, eventually killing more than 1,000 Athenians and capturing a further 2,000. For an Athenian contingent of, perhaps, 6,000 hoplites the losses were clearly high. The Thebans and their allies also suffered heavy losses and, in fact, the Sacred Band was never re-formed. It was in every sense a decisive Macedonian victory.

With Greece defenceless against the might of the Macedonian army, a meeting was called at Corinth where Philip sought to establish his leadership over Greece and unite the whole of Greece with Macedonia against the Persian Empire in retribution for the Persian invasions of the early 5th century BC. Although Sparta in her characteristic stubbornness refused to join, Macedonian hegemony over Greece following the battle of Chaeronea was now moot. Philip could turn to other conquests.

The Temple of Apollo at Corinth. In the summer of 337 BC, Philip II summoned the Greek leaders to Corinth in order to form a 'league', united, under his leadership, to bring retribution against Persia.

The assassination of Philip II

The security which Philip had brought to the Macedonian state, and which the crown prince, Alexander, was due to inherit, was to be disrupted by internal dynastic events. In 337 BC Philip took another wife, a Macedonian named Cleopatra. This raised the possibility of a fully Macedonian heir, a fact which her uncle, the powerful noble Attalus, was swift to note at the wedding party in the presence of both Philip and Alexander. Attalus had gravely insulted Alexander and, after the violent altercation which inevitably ensued, Alexander (as well as his mother, Olympias) went into exile. The marriage was certainly perceived as a direct threat to Alexander and further courtly intrigues likely added to a sense of increasing isolation for the young prince.

In 336 BC Philip had decided to marry one of his daughters to Olympias' brother, Alexander, king of Epirus, and it was at this wedding that Philip was assassinated by a disgruntled bodyguard, Pausanias. The 'official' explanation of the murder was that Pausanias, furious that Philip had refused to redress a serious and personal grievance that Pausanias had earlier had with Attalus, decided to kill the king. The details of this sordid event are impossible to unravel and conspiracy theories, ancient and modern, abound. Whether Alexander and Olympias (or others) were involved and what their motives might have been cannot be known. What is certain is that Alexander quickly seized the throne, eliminating potential rivals under various pretences and garnering the support, or at least co-operation, of other powerful figures, such as the generals Antipater and Parmenion.

By 335 BC, Alexander was firmly ensconced as the king of Macedon. He had received the acclamation of the army and had eliminated any rivals. Campaigning in Illyria, he finally subjugated the hill tribes there and, when Thebes revolted in early spring of that year, he savagely razed the city to the ground and enslaved the population. For the Greeks, the new king had set a clear and unequivocal example of the costs of rebellion. Following these campaigns, Alexander set out with the army for the invasion of Persia.

CHRONOLOGY

All dates BC

490	1st Persian invasion of Greece. Persian defeat at Marathon.
480	2nd Persian invasion of Greece. Spartan '300' defeated at Thermopylae. Athens sacked and burned. Greek naval victory off Salamis.
479	Persian army defeated at Plataea and navy defeated off Mycale.
449	Peace of Callias. Persia disavows future military intervention in mainland Greece.
431-401	Peloponnesian War. Athens defeated by Sparta and her empire dismantled.
401	The 'Ten Thousand' in Persia. The Greek mercenaries in support of the Persian usurper Cyrus operate in Asia Minor.
386	King's Peace. Spartan hegemony in Greece. Greek *poleis* of western Anatolia under Persian dominion.
362	Battle of 2nd Mantinea. Thebes and allies under Epiminondas defeat Sparta and allies, leading to Theban hegemony in Greece.
359	Accession of Philip II to the Macedonian throne.
356	Birth of Alexander III (the 'Great').
346	Isocrates produces his oration *Philippus*.
2 August 338	Battle of Chaeronea. Thebans and Athenians defeated by Philip and Alexander.
Summer 337	League of Corinth established. Macedonian hegemony recognized.
Summer 336	Accession of Darius III to the Persian throne.
Summer 336	Expedition force under Parmenion sent to Asia Minor.
October 336	Assassination of Philip II. Alexander accedes to the throne of Macedon.
October 336	Accession of Alexander III (the 'Great') to the Macedonian throne.
336/5	Illyrian campaign. Defeat of the Balkan hill tribes by Alexander.
335	Revolt of Thebes. The city is razed to the ground and the population enslaved by Alexander.
Spring 334	Alexander sets out from Aegae in Macedon with the invasion force.
Summer 334	Alexander visits Troy while Parmenion and the army cross the Hellespont.
May 334	Battle of the Granicus river (1st set battle against Persia).
Autumn 334	Siege of Halicarnassus.
Spring 333	Alexander cuts the Gordion Knot.
November 333	Battle of Issus (2nd set battle against Persia).
1 October 331	Battle of Gaugamela (3rd and final set battle against Persia).
Spring 330	Persepolis burned.
July 330	Death of Darius III.
May 326	Battle of Hydaspes river (modern Jhelum) against Porus.
10 June 323	Death of Alexander in Babylon.

OPPOSING COMMANDERS

MACEDONIAN

The career of Alexander the Great's father, Philip II, has been outlined in the introduction and his importance in the creation of the state and army of Macedonia which Alexander was to lead into Asia should not be underestimated. Alexander, of course, acceded to the kingship of Macedon with the acquiescence (or occasional removal) of the nobles and the acclamation of the army but those institutions inherited by Alexander which were so central to the military organization of the expedition into Asia, particularly the Companion Cavalry and Foot (i.e. infantry) Companions, had been restructured or created by Philip II. Furthermore, the consolidation of the Macedonian state in security and administrative matters, the increase in state revenues and economic development as well as the creation of the powerful army were all achievements of Philip II. As one scholar has succinctly summarized the relationship: 'No Philip, no Alexander' (Errington, 99).

This detail from the Alexander Sarcophagus discovered in Sidon (Lebanon) in 1887 shows Alexander in action against Persia. (akg-images/Erich Lessing)

Alexander III ('the Great')

In many respects, Alexander the Great is the subject of this book so only a cursory description of his career will be given here. He was born in 356 BC to Philip and his Molossian wife, Olympias. As a young man, one of his teachers was the eminent philosopher Aristotle. Alexander was regent of Macedon in Philip's absence during the campaign against Thrace and delivered the decisive blow in the battle of Chaeronea in 338 BC when he annihilated the Theban Sacred Band. Until Philip's marriage to the Macedonian Cleopatra and the possibility of a 'fully' Macedonian prince, Alexander was the recognised heir to the crown (his half-brother, Philip Arrhidaeus, was in some way mentally deficient).

Alexander swiftly assumed the kingship upon Philip's assassination, removing those potentially dangerous to him, such as Attalus, and securing the loyalty of those who supported him, such as Parmenion. Having consolidated his rule over Macedon he subdued the rebellious hill tribes of Illyria and crushed the revolt of Thebes which he razed to the ground as an example to the Greek *poleis*. He received his father's position as *hegemon* (leader) of the League of Corinth which had been established in 337 BC and began preparations in late 335 BC for the invasion of Persia.

In 334 BC this army crossed the Hellespont and met a local Persian army at the Granicus river. Alexander defeated this force and continued

This detail from a line drawing of the 'Alexander Mosaic' from the House of the Faun in Pompeii depicts Alexander at the battle of the Issus. The mosaic dates to the second half of the 2nd century BC but is believed to be a copy of a painting completed *c.* 330–310 BC.

18

down the Aegean coast of western Asia Minor, occupying (or 'liberating') the Greek *poleis,* formerly under Persian rule. By reducing these coastal cities he hoped to remove possible landing points for the powerful Persian navy, a strategy which was not fully realized until the capture of Egypt in 332 BC. At the battle of Issus in 333 BC he defeated the Persian army, this time under the personal leadership of Darius III. Alexander's ultimate triumph over Darius came at the battle of Gaugamela in 331 BC and by 330 BC the destruction of the Persian Empire was complete.

Further years of difficult campaigning through the eastern satrapies (provinces) of the Persian Empire followed and Alexander's eastern progress was eventually exhausted in the Punjab after his victory at the battle of the Hydaspes against a local Indian rajah, Porus, in 326 BC. He was unable to cajole his troops to campaign farther east and turned back to Babylon in 325 BC. Leading them down the Indus to the Indian Ocean and through the hostile terrain of the Gedrosian desert on the northern coast of the Persian Gulf, Alexander reached Babylon in 323 BC where he died of illness at 33 years of age.

Parmenion

Parmenion served as Alexander's second-in-command at the Granicus, commanding the left wing of the army as he would later do at the battle of Issus (333 BC) and Gaugamela (331 BC). This command was not new to Parmenion as he had served under Philip II in the same capacity, where he was so highly regarded it was said Philip remarked that 'in many years he himself had found only one general, Parmenion'. (Plutarch *Moralia* 177c).

This detail from the Alexander Sarcophagus shows a Companion cavalryman, perhaps an officer, in action against Persian infantry. Although of Philip's generation, the general Parmenion was a virtual second-in-command to Alexander. (akg-images/ Erich Lessing)

Parmenion's early origins and service are obscure but he was probably already in his 40s when he defeated the Illyrians in 356 BC (Plut. *Alex.* 3.8) and in 346 BC Parmenion was sent on the embassy to Athens which led to the Peace of Philocrates. In 336 BC he was sent with Attalus and Amnytas to lead the force of 10,000 which was to secure the bridgehead in Asia Minor ahead of the main invasion force. There he was only partially successful in his encounters against the Greek mercenary, Memnon of Rhodes, and the local Persian forces, suffering a defeat at Magnesia on the Meander, but he managed to establish a toehold in Asia Minor before his recall to Macedonia in the winter of 335 BC after the death of Philip.

Parmenion quickly associated himself with Alexander and acquiesced in the murder of the latter's potential rival Attalus, thereby helping Alexander to secure the throne. For this service he and his family were apparently well rewarded. In particular, his sons, Philotas and Nicanor, obtained major commands and fought at the Granicus: Philotas leading the Companion cavalry and Nicanor the infantry regiment known as the *hypaspists*.

At the Granicus, the historian Arrian (1.13.3–5) records that Parmenion advised Alexander to pitch camp and fight the next morning, a counsel which Alexander rejected in favour of immediate attack. In the battle, Parmenion held his usual role, commanding the Thessalian cavalry on the left wing where, according to Diodorus (17.19.6), they fought 'eagerly'. Parmenion continued his role as active 'second-in-command' until 330 BC when Alexander charged him with securing the captured treasure of Persia by moving it to Ecbatana.

Perhaps this was a reasonable posting for the aged veteran who was probably now in his 60s. Sadly, before the end of the year, he was killed by fellow Macedonians. Implicated in the alleged plot of his son, Philotas, against the king himself, Parmenion, in addition to his son, was sentenced to death. The details of this squalid affair are difficult to untangle but it is harsh to suggest that this capable, loyal and long-serving officer deserved such an ignominious end.

'Black' Cleitus

Cleitus, known in the ancient sources as 'Black' Cleitus, to distinguish him from a lesser Cleitus of the later Alexander campaigns, was born of Macedonian nobility (his sister, Lanice, had served as Alexander's wet-nurse) and he served in the Companion Cavalry under Philip and Alexander. At the decisive battle of Gaugamela in 331 BC, Cleitus commanded the *ile basilike* ('Royal squadron'), also known as the *agema*, the king's personal mounted bodyguard of Companions, and it is likely that he held this command at the battle of the Granicus River. Moreover, despite discrepancies in details, the ancient historians agree that he saved Alexander's life at the Granicus when he severed the arm of a Persian satrap who was poised to give Alexander the fatal *coup-de-grace*.

In 330 BC when the cavalry was re-formed into two *hipparchies*, Cleitus held joint command with Alexander's closest companion, Hephaestion (Heckel, 35–6). In the course of the next two years, Cleitus performed valuable service during the tough guerrilla warfare in Persia's north-eastern provinces. None the less, in one of the most dramatic events in the whole of the Alexander story, Cleitus was murdered by a frenzied

Alexander at a drinking party in the autumn of 328 BC. The excessive flattery offered to Alexander by obsequious courtiers and the implicit and explicit denigration of Philip and Philip's commanders at the banquet offended Cleitus who in turn praised Philip and his generation's accomplishments. Perceiving this as an insult in the extreme, the incensed and drunken Alexander promptly ran him through with a lance. The king's later remorse hardly expiates what was one of his blackest moments.

PERSIAN

In the 4th century BC, the Persian Empire, the rulers of which were called by the Greeks the *megas basileus*, or Great King, was the largest ever seen in the ancient Near East. Under the capable leadership of the Achaemenid dynasty founded by Cyrus II in 559 BC, who unified Media and Persia, Persian holdings, by the time of Alexander's invasion, extended from the shores of western Anatolia to the Indus Valley in the east and from Bactria (modern Afghanistan) in the north to the southern cataracts of the River Nile in Egypt. From the reign of Darius I (521–485 BC) the Empire was ruled from the capital Persepolis through a structure of administrative units known as *satrapies* (provinces).

The *satraps* (governors) who administered these districts were principally responsible for yearly tribute remitted to the central government and, with the help of a military overseer, raising forces for the army. However, they were granted a great degree of autonomy in return for protecting the kingdom. Despite, or perhaps because of this autonomy, the satraps at times proved themselves somewhat less than loyal to the Great King. Rebellions occurred, particularly in the 360s BC in Asia Minor when a number of now virtually hereditary satraps attempted to carve out essentially independent kingdoms. In addition, rivals and usurpers to the throne also emerged from satrapal ranks, as in the case of Cyrus the Younger who in 401 BC, leading an army with the '10,000' Greek mercenaries immortalized in Xenophon's *Anabasis*, failed in his attempt to seize the Persian throne of Artaxerxes after perishing in the battle of Cunaxa.

The Persian satraps and other commanders

Darius III, who himself had only gained the throne of Persia in 336 BC, relied on the satraps and nobles of Asia Minor to meet the Macedonian incursion. They were better placed for the initial engagement and he did not personally lead the army until the battles of Issus (333 BC) and Gaugamela (331 BC) when Alexander had penetrated much deeper into the Persian heartland.

The Persian commanders met for a war council at Zeleia roughly 20 miles east of the river Granicus. The ancient historians provide names for 14 of the commanders. Of these, five were satraps of provinces in Asia Minor: Arsames of Cilicia, Arsites of Hellespontine Phrygia, Atizyes of Greater Phrygia, Mithrobuzanes of Cappadocia, and Spithridates of Lydia and Ionia. Little is known of these men personally, but Diodorus (17.19.4) records that they led various regional cavalry units at the battle. Mithrobuzanes and Spithridates were killed in the battle, the latter at the

The Persian Commanders at Granicus

Name	Command
Arbupales (son of Darius, son of Artaxerxes II)	
Arsames	Cilicia (satrap)
Arsites	Hellespontine Phrygia (*hyparch* and satrap)
Atizyes	Greater Phrygia (satrap)
Memnon (Greek mercenary)	Held estates in the Troad
Mithridates (son-in-law of Darius)	
Mithrobuzanes	Southern Cappadocia (*hyparch* and satrap)
Niphates	A landowner in Asia Minor
Omares (commander of the mercenaries)	
Petenes	A landowner in Asia Minor
Pharances (brother of Darius' wife)	
Rheomithres	
Rhoesaces (brother of Spithridates)	
Spithridates (brother of Rhoesaces)	Lydia and Ionia (satrap)

hand of Alexander. Atizyes fled and was killed at the battle of Issus, while no mention is made of the fate of Arsames. Intriguingly, Arrian (1.16.3) says that Arsites committed suicide after fleeing the battlefield because the Persians blamed him for the defeat, perhaps because he opposed Memnon's counsel not to face Alexander immediately.

Eight other Persians and Memnon, the Rhodian mercenary commander, are also named as present at the battle. Three relations of Darius fought and died in the battle: Arbupales, Mithridates, and Pharnaces, while the brother of Spithridates, Rhoesaces, was at least severely wounded. Of the remainder, Niphates, Petenes and Omares (perhaps a Persian who commanded the Greek mercenary infantry) perished in the battle, while no mention is made of the fate of Rheomithres. Memnon, who held estates in the Troad, also escaped.

Thus, of the 14 named commanders, eight are noted as having died in battle with at least one severely wounded, a rather high casualty rate for the Persian nobility who can by no means be considered cowardly.

Memnon of Rhodes

Memnon, and his brother Mentor, had served the Persians as mercenary commanders in the Troad from at least the 350s BC. Connections between the Rhodian brothers and the local satrap were evidently very close. Mentor had married Barsine, the sister of Aratabazus, the satrap of Lower (or Hellespontine) Phrygia (north-western Anatolia), who in turn had married one of the Rhodians' sisters. When Artabazus failed in his rebellion against Artaxerxes III ('Ochus') in 353 or 352 BC they were forced into exile at Pella in Macedonia.

Their capabilities as military commanders were still, however, highly valued and Mentor was pardoned by the Great King in 343 BC, whereupon he subjugated the province of Egypt which had freed itself from Persian control 60 years earlier. In return for this service, Memnon and Artabazus were also allowed to return. Upon Mentor's death in 340 BC, Memnon was granted his lands and military authority, and even married his brother's widow, Barsine.

Memnon was tasked with countering Parmenion's advance force, which had been sent to the coast of Asia Minor in 336 BC, and he was largely successful in forcing the Macedonian incursion back to the Troad and Hellespont region. However, in 335 BC he was unable to completely eject the advance force from Asia, which was soon to be joined by the main army under Alexander.

When the satraps gathered at Zeleia to formulate their strategy to combat Alexander, Memnon counselled a delaying 'scorched earth' policy to exhaust the resources available to the Macedonian army. Perhaps out of an innate distrust of the Greek, the satraps rejected this advice and met Alexander at the Granicus River. Memnon was active in the battle but, unlike the Greek mercenaries and many Persian satraps, he fled the field and escaped.

Despite the defeat at the Granicus, Memnon was put in charge of the defence of western Asia Minor and organised the tenacious defence of Halicarnassus which was besieged at a cost by Alexander in 333 BC. After control of the western Anatolian seaboard fell to Alexander, Memnon collected a large fleet and operated in the Aegean, seizing islands and cities and threatening Alexander's rear. The potential for disrupting Alexander's progress east created by these operations was significant, and they even drew interest from Greek *poleis* such as Sparta who foresaw a chance to join forces and throw off the Macedonian yoke. At the siege of Mytilene in 333 BC, however, Memnon fell ill and died. With the threat of this capable commander removed, Alexander was able to continue his campaign with his supply lines and Greek 'allies' safe and intact.

OPPOSING ARMIES

MACEDONIA AND HER ALLIES

I n 326 BC Alexander's eastward march was brought to a halt by the 'mutiny' of his troops at the River Hyphasis (the modern Beas in eastern Pakistan). Alexander addressed the army and, in recalling how his father, Philip, had changed Macedon said:

> *he made you a match in battle for the barbarians on your borders, so that you no longer trusted for your safety to the strength of your positions so much as to your natural courage... It was due to him that you became masters and not slaves and subjects of those very barbarians who used previously to plunder your possessions and carry off your persons (Arr. 7.9.2).*

Philip had done this by reorganizing, equipping and training an army that the Greeks previously had looked upon as little more than a rabble. At the end of his life, Philip had 'left armies so numerous and powerful that his son Alexander had no need to apply for allies in his attempt to overthrow the Persian supremacy.' (Diod. 16.1.5)

Macedonian infantry

A significant part of the reorganization was the creation of a formidable infantry phalanx (Diod. 16.3.2). From 10,000 infantry in 359 BC the infantry had grown to at least 24,000 by 334 BC and they had the technical advantage of being equipped with a long pike (*sarissa*), roughly 5–6m (*c.* 15–18 feet) in length. Made of cornel wood and tipped with an iron spear tip at front and iron butt at rear, the *sarissa* was roughly twice the length of the traditional thrusting spear of the Greek hoplite. Although the length of *sarissa* required the use of both hands, and thus necessitated the lightening of a defensive shield to one resting on the shoulder held by a sling over the neck and a forearm strap on the shield, its extended length was advantageous in keeping opposing infantry at bay. In a phalanx the spear tips of the levelled *sarissae* of the first three to four ranks would project beyond the front rank while the remaining ranks would hold their *sarissae* upright or inclined to the front to protect against missile attack. This bristling front of spear points prevented opposing infantry from making initial contact with the Macedonians, an enormous advantage in this type of hand-to-hand combat. As well as the small shield, defensive armour also included a helmet, a linen cuirass, and greaves.

For a unit of men to manipulate the *sarissa* effectively, a high degree of training was necessary to maintain cohesion. Philip initiated constant and rigorous manoeuvres and drills (Diod. 16.3.1) which honed his infantry to a degree of professionalism rarely matched in Greece. Moreover, much like the Roman general Marius' 'mules', each soldier carried his own equipment and rations, and was physically trained to endure long and swift marches. This ability to move quickly and over great distances was a strategic advantage well used by Philip and Alexander.

The infantry were named the 'foot-companions' (*pezetairoi*) in conscious imitation of the land-owning cavalrymen known simply as the 'companions' (*hetaroi*) and at the time of the battle of the Granicus the *pezetairoi* were marshalled in six *taxeis* ('brigades' or 'battalions') of 1,500 men each, recruited to some extent regionally. In addition, another elite infantry formation known as the 'shield-bearers' (*hypaspists*), numbering three units of 1,000 men (whether equipped as the 'foot-companions' or like the Greek hoplite is a matter of considerable debate), constituted the full Macedonian phalanx (Heckel and Jones, 17–18). The *hypaspists* were under the command of Nicanor, a son of Parmenion. In total, Alexander had 12,000 heavy Macedonian infantry at the battle of the Granicus.

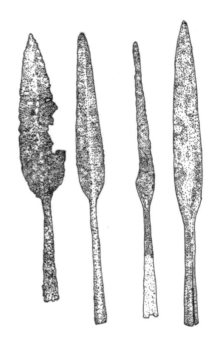

Examples of Macedonian sarissa spear points excavated from the royal tombs at Vergina. Drawn from a photo by Ph. Petsas.

Macedonian cavalry

If the Macedonian phalanx was the 'anvil' used to fix the opposing phalanx, then the 'hammer' was the cavalry. As early as 359 BC, when 600 cavalry are accounted in the battle against the Illyrian king Bardylis, cavalry was used in co-ordination with infantry (Diod. 16.4.4–5). This indicates that a tradition of combined arms was well established before Alexander's tactical refinements created his major victories. By the time of Alexander's accession the number of Macedonian cavalry had risen to 3,300. Of these he left 1,500 with a sizeable infantry force under the command of Antipater to protect the Macedonian homeland and to keep a wary eye on his Greek 'allies' and Balkan neighbours.

Of the 5,100 cavalry that crossed the Hellespont in the invasion force, 1,800 were Macedonian (Diod. 17.17.4). This force, the 'Companion cavalry', was the principal striking force of the army and was formed into eight 'squadrons' (*ilai*, singular *ile*), one of which was the 'Royal' squadron (the *agema* or *ile basilike*) often led by the king himself. If, as is generally thought, the Royal squadron would have a

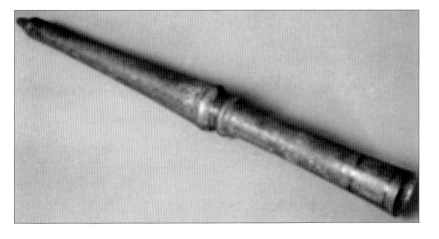

This is a rare example of a spear-butt from a Macedonian *sarissa*. When cleaned, the letters 'M A K' standing for 'Mac[edonian]' were revealed. The style of the letters dates the item to the later 4th century BC. (Shefton Museum, University of Newcastle)

strength of around 300, the regular *ilai* would have had nominal strength of roughly 200 (Milns, 167; cf. Brunt, 39–41). The Companion cavalry was under the overall command of Philotas, a son of Parmenion.

The Companion cavalry were armed with a lance (*xyston*), shorter than the infantry *sarissa* but still roughly 2.5–3.5m (*c.* 7–10 feet) in length (following Manti and Gaebel, 172 *contra* Markle [1978 and 1979]) and, according to the pictorial evidence of the so-called 'Alexander' mosaic found in Pompeii, it could be handled with one arm without difficulty. The cavalry also carried a short slashing sword and were equipped with Boeotian-style helmets and corselets although not shields.

Another force of cavalry, the 'scouts' or 'lancers' (*prodromoi*), were probably also ethnic Macedonians (Brunt, 27-8). The exact unit strength of the *prodromoi* is not known. However, if we accept Plutarch's comment (*Alex.* 16.4) that 13 'squadrons' crossed the Granicus with Alexander, one has to assume that four of these were 'lancers' (i.e. less than 8 'squadrons' of Companions and the single Paeonian squadron). Now since Diodorus says (17.17.4) that the total Thracian, *prodromoi*, and Paeonian cavalry amounted to 900 at the crossing, we have to conclude that a 'lancer' squadron was smaller than a Companion squadron. The figures suggest that it was not much more than 100 troopers.

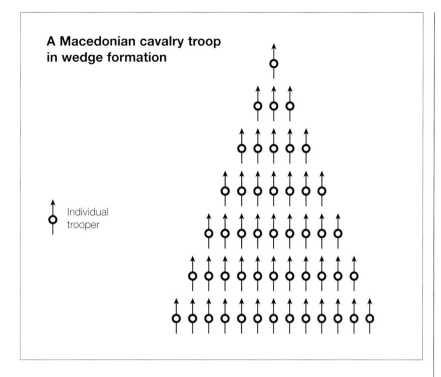

A Macedonian cavalry troop in wedge formation

Individual trooper

We do know that the 'lancers' were armed with a cavalry '*sarissa*' because they are sometimes referred to as 'sarissa bearers' (*sarissophoroi*). Although it must have been shorter than the infantry *sarissa* it still probably required the use of two hands and thus would have required a very skilled horseman to manipulate both it and the horse.

Allied cavalry

Perhaps as significant as the Companion cavalry, were the 1,800-strong Thessalian cavalry which fought at the Granicus under the overall command of Parmenion on the left wing. Thessaly had historically been horse-rearing country and the Thessalian cavalry was regarded as among the finest in Greece. When Philip was elected *tagus* of the Thessalian league in 352 BC, following his victory at the battle of Crocus Field, he received the use of this effective fighting force, which Alexander also significantly used in his three major victories against Persia.

As well as the Thessalians, a contingent of 600 Greek cavalry under the command of Philip, son of Menelaus, and a 300-strong unit of Thracian cavalry under Agathon formed the left wing at the Granicus. Supporting the Companions on the right wing were units of Paeonian cavalry and the *prodromoi*. These last two, as well as Socrates' *ile* of the Companion cavalry and some light infantry, formed the 'advance guard' led by Amyntas which initiated the battle.

Light infantry

Like their neighbours the Paeonians, the Agrianian javelin-men hailed from the mountainous regions north of Upper Macedonia. This unit, numbering 500, was highly valued by Alexander and was used in some of the toughest engagements fought in the campaign. At the battle of the Granicus they fought amongst the cavalry during the crossing of the

Head of Alexander from the Archaeological Museum, Istanbul. It was found during excavations at Pergamum. Although this head dates to the first half of the 2nd century BC the style is typical of Alexander's court sculptor, Lysippus.

river, unlike the traditional role of light-armed skirmishers who so often in ancient warfare launched their missiles to open the battle but retired to safety before the main engagement of heavy infantry. At the Granicus, the 500 Cretan archers who screened the cavalry on the right wing may have played this more traditional skirmishing role.

Command structure

Macedonian kingship was pure monarchy and Alexander would have appreciated Louis XIV's famous dictum *'l'État c'est moi'*. Overall command of the armed forces was simply another undisputed element of a king's role as the head of Macedonia, such as minting coinage or making treaties in his name alone. Nevertheless, the Macedonian nobility were not to be run roughshod over and they played a vital role within military command.

Parmenion, Philip's valued general, was virtually the overall second-in-command, and held the commanding position on the left of the Macedonian battle line at the Granicus, as well as at Issus and Gaugamela. His son, Philotas, also held the prestigious position of commander of the Companion cavalry while another son, Nicanor, commanded the hypaspists.

The sources also indicate a fairly thorough chain of command with most units having named commanders. Each of the phalanx battalions have a named commander with distinguishing patronymic (Meleager, Philip, Amyntas, Craterus, Coenus, and Perdiccas) as well as the 3,000-strong elite 'shield-bearers' (Nicanor, son of Parmenion). The Greek allied cavalry and Thracian cavalry at the Granicus were commanded by Philip, son of Menelaus, and Agathon respectively. Amyntas, son of Arrhabaeus, commanded the advance guard of Agrianian, Paeonian cavalry, *prodromoi*, and the Companion squadron of Socrates, son of Sathon (Arr. 1 .12.7).

PERSIANS AND THEIR GREEK MERCENARIES

Under the Achaemenids, the army of the peoples of the Iranian plateau developed significantly. Earlier in Media, the army, known in Old Persian as the *spâda*, was first organized into distinct units at the end of the 7th century BC by the Median king, Cyaxares (Herodotus *Histories* 1.103). The Medes, amongst others, were superseded and united with Persia, their eastern neighbours, by Cyrus the Great in the 6th century BC. Medes and Persians formed the core of the *spâda* although other subjugated peoples, such as the Hyrcanians and Bactrians, who appear at the Granicus, were also incorporated into the army, using their native weapons, skills and techniques. Persia was also keen to make use of Greek mercenaries whose superiority as heavy infantry was learned at first hand in the Graeco-Persian wars of the early 5th century BC.

Persian cavalry

Native Persian military strength lay in their cavalry. The horse stocks of Nisea provided the finest ponies in the ancient Near East and from a young age the nobility were trained in horsemanship (Sekunda, 54).

Herodotus (1.136) claimed that from the age of five to 20 young men were taught, 'only three things: riding and archery and honesty'. Expertise at the hunt and its associated skills of archery and throwing a spear transferred easily to the military sphere. On an inscription at Naqs-e Rostam, Darius the Great proclaimed the values of the Persian nobility: 'As a horseman I am a good horseman. As a bowman I am a good bowman both afoot and on horseback. As a spearman I am a good spearman both afoot and on horseback.' (Kent, 140).

Persian cavalry were armed and equipped in a variety of ways (Herodotus 7.61.1). However, at the battle of the Granicus, the Persian cavalry were equipped with two spears (*palta*) one of which, most likely, was for throwing, the other for stabbing. Mounted archers are not attested at the battle and the cavalry were not armed with shields. Their clothing consisted of tight fitting trousers made of textile (or possibly leather); a girdle holding a short sword (*acinces*); a long, tight fabric tunic with long sleeves; and a round felt headpiece with cheek, neck and mouth coverings.

Sculptural relief of two Medes from the Persian Royal palace at Persepolis. Medes and Persians formed the core populations of the Persian Empire. (Jona Lendering, www.livius.org)

Persian infantry would have been similarly armed and equipped. The short sword, spear composed of wooden shaft with metal head and butt, bow and quiver, and wicker shield were common. However, Persian infantry did not fight at the battle of the Granicus. Their role was taken by the Greek mercenary hoplites who are described below and who were regularly hired by the satraps of western Anatolia. At the battle of the Granicus the Persian cavalry numbered around 10,000 and played a principal role in the battle.

Persian military organization

We know from a deposit of baked clay cuneiform fortification tablets excavated at Persepolis that the Persian military was organized on the decimal system. The smallest unit was known as a *dathabam* (roughly equivalent to a company) and larger units of 100 (*satabam*), 1,000 (*hazarabam*) and 10,000 (*baivarabam*) men were composed from these units (Sekunda, 5). Each of these divisions had a commander and ultimately the whole of the army (*spâda*) was led by the *spâdapati*, usually the Great King himself or a close associate. The Greeks sometimes called the head of the Persian army, *karanos*, a translation of the Old Persian *kârana*, leader of 'the army' and originally, by metonomy, leader of the *kâra*, i.e. 'the people' in general.

As supreme commanders, Persian kings were often present at, even participating in, battles. However, for reasons which will be examined later, Darius III was not present at the battle of the Granicus and he delegated the command of his forces not to a *spâdapati* or *karanos* but rather to a council of regional satraps and the Rhodian mercenary commander, Memnon. It has been suggested that Arsites, the satrap of Hellespontine Phrygia (through which the Granicus flows) had overall

responsibility for the Persian force at the Granicus (Briant, 821–3), but there is no direct evidence of this. Scholars disagree as to whether there was an overall commander-in-chief at the Granicus, or whether it was leadership 'by committee' (Davis, 44). Although the evidence is ultimately indecisive, this book argues that Arsites held a role something akin to a *primus inter pares* or 'first among equals'.

Although, with a single exception, tactical decisions made by the Persians during the battle are not attributed to individual commanders in the ancient sources, the traditional war council to discuss strategy, held at Zeleia before the battle of the Granicus, was noted (Arr. 1.12.8–10; Diod. 17.18.2–4).

Greek mercenaries

From at the least the middle of the 5th century BC, Persia made extensive use of Greek mercenaries, usually in the form of personal bodyguards for provincial chiefs and garrisons for the Greek cities of western Asia Minor. In the 4th century BC increasing numbers of mercenaries were employed by the western satraps and figured prominently in their periodic revolts against the Great King. The most notable example was Cyrus' '10,000' which he hired in his attempt to usurp the throne of Artaxerxes in 401 BC. Like the Swiss mercenaries of early modern Europe, great numbers of mainland Greek mercenaries were recruited from the mountainous regions of the Peloponnese, although their commanders came from all areas of Greece. As we have seen, Memnon, who advised and commanded at the Granicus, originally came from Rhodes and it is certain that many mercenaries were recruited by the Persians from the local Greek populations of Asia Minor. There is evidence that some of the Greek mercenaries at the Granicus hailed from Athens, Thebes and even Thessaly (Arr. 1.29.5; 3.6.2, cf. Plutarch, *Sayings of Alexander* 181a–b). Alexander's relations with Athens and Thebes were largely hostile so it is

perhaps not too surprising to find members of these *poleis* fighting in Persian pay against him.

The Greek hoplite – heavily armed with greaves, breastplate, shield (the *hoplon* or *aspis*), helmet, thrusting spear, and short sword – was the pre-eminent heavy infantry of the classical Greek world before the arrival of the Macedonian phalanx. Operating in a packed phalanx formation, they had shown that they could defeat levies of more lightly armed eastern infantry. By the 4th century BC the traditional clash of hoplite phalanxes had given way to more sophisticated combined-arms combat, using lighter armed *peltasts*, specialist skirmishing troops, and, ever increasingly, cavalry. Nevertheless, the Greek hoplite was still highly regarded and formed the bulk of the mercenaries in Persian service.

Arrian (1.14.1) claims that at the battle of the Granicus 20,000 mercenaries were present but this figure seems too high. We know that Memnon headed a force of 5,000 mercenaries during his campaign against Parmenion's advance force in 335 BC (Diod. 17.7.3, cf. Polyaenus 5.44.4 '4,000' mercenaries) and it will be argued that this is a more likely figure for the mercenaries at the Granicus.

Modern historians have often placed Persian or 'native' Asian infantry at the battle and this may be an attempt to account for the incredibly high infantry figure given by Diodorus ('100,000', 17.19.5, cf. Justin's [11.6] absurd '600,000'!). However, there is no need to account for what is certainly an erroneously high number of 'Persian' infantry by postulating native infantry in addition to the Greek mercenaries. It is simpler and more coherent to assume that only Greek mercenaries, and only a relatively small force, were present.

31

OPPOSING PLANS

MACEDONIAN PLANS

I t is not clear when Philip II formulated his plans for the invasion of Persia. As we have seen, the rhetorician Isocrates had been urging the Greeks to unify and launch a pan-Hellenic 'crusade' against Persia as early as the 380s BC when he wrote the oration, *Panegyricus.* Although Athens and Sparta, and later the tyrants Alexander and Jason of Pherae, baulked at assuming the leadership Isocrates urged, when Philip came to prominence, the rhetorician did not hesitate to produce in 346 BC the pamphlet *Philippus*, in the form of an open letter, exhorting Philip to lead the expedition. However, it is unknown what effect, if any, this had on him.

Some scholars have suggested that Philip had his 'Persian plans' firmly in mind as early as 348 BC although this is doubtful. Indeed, in the decade from 348–338 BC, Philip still had his hands full in completely gaining the support of Thessaly, pacifying the Greek states to the south, and securing the route to Asia via the Hellespont through the volatile lands of Thrace. It is more likely that he fully and finally turned his attention to Persia after the battle of Chaeronea when these objectives had been achieved. According to Diodorus (16.89.2), shortly before the meeting which established the League of Corinth in 337 BC, Philip was making known throughout Greece his desire to attack Persia 'to punish them for the profanation of the temples' in the Graeco-Persian wars.

Philip's leniency in dealing with Athens after Chaeronea has been explained by suggesting that he desired their co-operation in an expedition against Persia. In particular he would require the use of the Athenian fleet as the Macedonian navy was relatively deficient and no match for a powerful Persian fleet operating in the Aegean. In any event he made little use of the fleet or, in fact, of his Greek allies as military assets during the campaign. Any concept of a pan-Hellenic 'crusade' was clearly subordinated to Macedonian hegemony and the ancient historian Polybius (3.6) maintained that Asia was attacked because Philip and Alexander believed it was weak – simply another ripe picking for their military machine and meat for their voracious appetite for expansion.

However, there were 'official' *causi belli* offered for the campaign. One of these, as we have seen, was to avenge the sacrilegious desecration of Greece at the hands of Persia during the Persian invasions of 490 and 480–79 BC. Alexander did claim to have burned the palace at Persepolis in 330 BC for this very reason (Arr. 3.18.12) and, after the battle of the Granicus, he did dedicate captured equipment for the Athenian Acropolis as partial recompense for their suffering during these wars (Arr. 1.16.7; Plut. *Alex.* 16.8). Of more immediate concern, perhaps, was

Sculptural relief of a Thracian from the Persian Royal city of Persepolis. Macedon was often in conflict with the tribes of Thrace and Alexander was forced to campaign there in 336/5 BC. (Jona Lendering, www.livius.org)

the subject status of the Greek cities of Asia Minor. These *poleis* had been under Persian suzerainty since the King's Peace of 386 BC settled by Sparta and Persia. The stated desire for freedom and autonomy for Greeks was an oft bandied excuse for military intervention in Greek affairs throughout the 5th and 4th centuries BC and Diodorus has Alexander making this very claim shortly after the battle of the Granicus (Diod. 17.24.1).

Whether these explanations were mere pretexts for a massive land-grab or genuine and deeply held beliefs depends on one's view of Alexander and his relationship with the Greeks and his fellow Macedonians. What does seem certain, however, is that once the invasion was underway, Alexander was eager and determined to make contact with the enemy as soon as possible.

PERSIAN PLANS

The failure of the Persians to contest Alexander's entry into Asia is perhaps not as surprising as it first appears. The newly installed king Darius had other priorities which immediately concerned him; such as the possibility of satrapal revolts, unrest in the northern province of Cadusia, and quashing rebellion in Egypt (Garvin, 91–94). Greek affairs were usually handled diplomatically, largely through bribery, and Greek military incursions could be dealt with by the western satraps and hired Greek mercenaries. Despite their earlier encounters, and the Persian

Detail from the Alexander Mosaic of the Persian Great King, Darius III. Darius was not present at the Granicus in 334 BC but led the Persian army at the battle of Issus the following year. (Alinari)

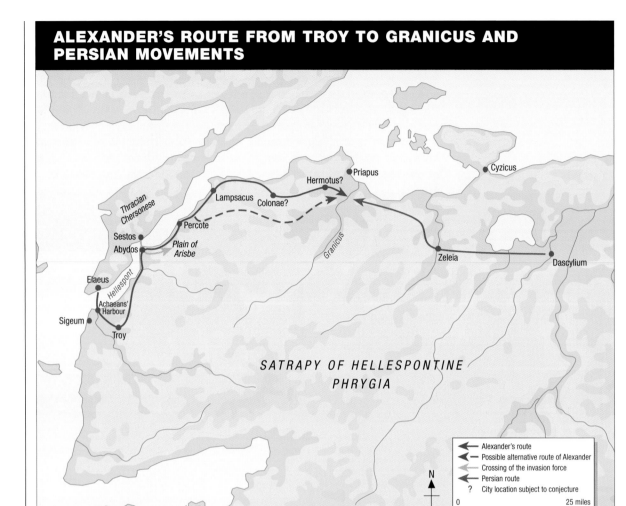

defeats suffered in the 5th century BC, the Greek world to the west must have registered only on the periphery of the world-view of the Great King, who ruled over a vast empire of nations. By the 4th century BC, Persia, much like Rome in the 2nd century AD, had ceased expanding and was content to secure its empire.

Nevertheless, Darius would have been aware of the invasion and begun preparations to counter the incursion even if he was not yet able, or deemed it necessary, to lead the opposition in person (Garvin, 97; Briant, 819). The immediate task of engaging the Macedonians was left to the Persian satraps of western Asia Minor who were best placed to deal with Alexander's expedition. In May 334 BC, these satraps and the their mercenary commander Memnon gathered at the city of Zeleia roughly 20 miles east of the River Granicus, where the Persian cavalry and the mercenary Greek infantry had assembled. The ancient historians Arrian (1.12.8-10) and Diodorus (17.18.2-4) both report a Persian war council at Zeleia and this meeting offers a fascinating insight into Persian strategic thinking regarding how to confront Alexander's incipient invasion.

At the council, Memnon argued that it was preferable for the Persians to avoid a pitched battle with Alexander and rather adopt scorched-earth tactics. On the one hand, the Macedonians, he stated, had much greater numbers of infantry and on the other, were short of supplies. This advice was rejected by Arsites, the satrap of Hellespontine Phrygia – the territory in which Alexander had landed and where the battle would take place. Arsites would not allow his land to be burned and, it seems, the other Persian satraps agreed with his rejection of Memnon's cautious advice, either as being beneath their dignity or out of suspicion of the Greek's motives. Memnon's advice may be a later addition by the Greek historians to highlight hubris on the part of Persians refusing sound Greek advice, but it was in the general remit of a satrap to protect the land he governed on behalf of the Great King (Briant 820–2). Alexander, as far as the Persians were concerned, was an unknown quantity in 334 BC and their decision to confront him as soon as he had entered their empire is difficult to condemn.

CAMPAIGN

THE ANCIENT SOURCES

Before we consider in detail the course of events of the campaign and battle of the Granicus River it is important to examine the evidence upon which any reconstruction, this one included, is ultimately based. Four literary sources provide the bulk of the evidence for the battle and these narratives are characterized by two important facts. First, these authors wrote anywhere from three to five centuries after the battle itself, a great chronological distance from the events. Secondly, these sources often, and on occasion very significantly, diverge in their testimonies of what occurred. In order to reconcile their accounts, or privilege elements of one account over another, it is necessary to consider the nature and veracity of these narratives.

Arrian of Nicomedia wrote a *History of Alexander* in the first half of the 2nd century AD. A native of the Bithynian city of Nicomedia in western Asia Minor, he served in a number of high-ranking capacities in the Roman administration of Asia Minor during the reign of the emperor Hadrian. As legate of Cappadocia he oversaw the defeat of the barbarian Alan incursion in 135 AD and wrote a work entitled, *The Order of Battle against the Alans*, which sheds early light on the arrangement and fighting techniques of the Roman army. Arrian modelled himself on the 4th century BC writer Xenophon, who wrote about 4th-century BC Greek history and was an experienced military commander himself.

Arrian's *History of Alexander* is often taken to be the most trustworthy account of Alexander's career, largely because he used sources, Ptolemy and Aristobulus, who were contemporaries of Alexander and participants in his campaigns. In the introduction to his history, Arrian remarks that, '...in my view Ptolemy and Aristobulus are more trustworthy in their narrative [than other writers], since Aristobulus took part in king Alexander's expedition, and Ptolemy...did the same...' (Arr. preface). This use of contemporary sources and his detailed and consistent style has seen Arrian's *History* highly valued amongst scholars, even though he has had his detractors. In fact, his account of the battle of the Granicus is usually regarded as the best of those which have come down to us.

Nevertheless, two other Alexander sources, Diodorus Siculus' *Library of History* in book 17 and Plutarch's *Life of Alexander* also contain descriptions of the battle. Diodorus wrote his account of Alexander in the last half of the 1st century BC and is a member of what modern scholars term the 'vulgate' tradition because he, like others, made use of Cleitarchus, who some time around 300 BC wrote an account of Alexander's campaign based on first-hand accounts. Diodorus is often thought of as an uncritical compiler of earlier historians who simply stitched their versions of events into a 'universal' history, but this view is now seen as unnecessarily harsh.

Plutarch also made use of Cleitarchus, as well as many other sources, in his *Life of Alexander*. A native of Chaeronea, like Arrian he served in the Roman provincial administration (in his native Greece) in the late 1st century AD. He was a prolific author writing on philosophy, morals, rhetoric, and biography. Plutarch's *Life of Alexander* fits squarely in the latter genre and contains definite moralizing tendencies and interesting anecdotal tales. Despite the difficulties in both Diodorus' and Plutarch's approach to history, both accounts are an important counterbalance to Arrian's sometimes sanitized and certainly court-centred history of Alexander.

Justin's *Epitome of the Universal History of Pompeius Trogus* also contains a brief account of the battle of the Granicus. Some time around 200 AD, Justin abridged an earlier work of 'universal' history written in Latin by Pompeius Trogus, a native of southern Gaul (modern southern France). Justin's abridgement seems as severe and rhetorically charged as it later proved popular, and appears to belong to the same 'vulgate' tradition emanating from Cleitarchus, from which Diodorus and Plutarch borrowed. However, what little detail it does provide about the battle is worth considering in conjunction with the others.

ABOVE **This coin depicts Ptolemy I 'Soter' who established the Ptolemaic dynasty which ruled Egypt until Cleopatra and Mark Antony's defeat at Actium in 31 BC. Ptolemy was an officer in Alexander's army and his first-hand history of the campaign was later used by Arrian. (akg-images/ Erich Lessing)**

Historical sources for the battle of the Granicus

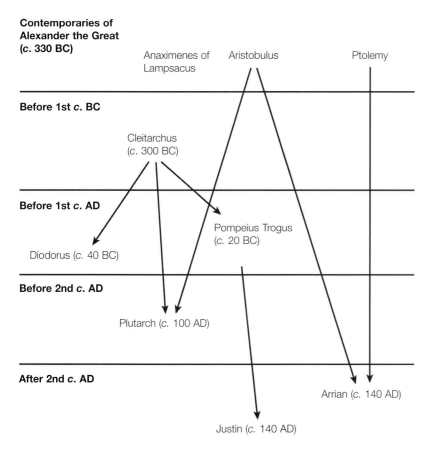

LEFT **This diagram indicates when the ancient historians of Alexander composed their works and the sources they used. In this simplified diagram, only authors cited in this book and relevant to the Granicus campaign are noted.**

Preparations for the invasion

Whenever Philip's invasion plans were actually formulated, by 336 BC they were being implemented. In that year he sent an advance force of 10,000 soldiers under the command of two senior generals, Parmenion and Attalus, to 'liberate' the cities of western Asia Minor in preparation for the full-scale invasion. This force established control from the Hellespont to Ephesus before they were rolled back in 335 BC by a 5,000-strong mercenary force under the Rhodian *condottiere*, Memnon. Memnon was able to force the Macedonians out of Ephesus, Magnesia on the Sipylus and Lampsacus but was eventually rebuffed in his attempt to take Cyzicus. Despite the advance force's uneven success in this initial stage, a vital bridgehead in Asia had been secured and maintained until 334 BC.

Following the assassination of Philip and the accession of Alexander, Thebes, which had revolted, and discontented elements in Thrace, had to be finally subjugated. Once this was completed in 335 BC, Alexander set out with the army for the great expedition against the Persian Empire. The historian Plutarch (*Alex.* 5.4) recorded that even as a young boy, Alexander expressed concern that his father would not leave him any great deeds to achieve and there is no reason to doubt that this expedition was foremost in his plans. Now he was able to lead a formidable and battle-hardened army into Persia and he set out by following the route which Xerxes had used in the invasion of Greece a century-and-a-half earlier.

The march to the Hellespont

Before joining the army, which was perhaps mustered at Therme near

A view of the extensive remains of Persepolis, a royal residence of the Achaemenid kings who ruled Persia from 559–330 BC. The vast complex is indicative of the grandeur and power of the Persian Empire until its demise at the hands of Alexander and his army. (Alinari)

The Hellespont between Sestos, located on the left (western) shore, and Abydos, on the right (eastern) shore was where Parmenion ferried the Macedonian army into Asia.

modern Thessoloniki, Alexander held games and made sacrifices to the Muses and Zeus (Engels, 26–7). After this the army set out along the southern coast of Thrace, bypassing Lake Cercinitis, heading towards the town of Amphipolis which crossed the River Strymon. From Amphipolis he passed Mt Pangaion, heading east towards the Greek city foundations of Abdera and Maronea on the coast of the north Aegean. Crossing the River Hebrus, the army traversed the Thracian region of the Paetice tribe. At the western point of the Chersonese, Alexander led the army across the 'Black' river. Twenty days and over 300 miles after setting out from Macedonia, the army had reached Sestos in the Thracian Chersonese (Gallipoli peninsula) on the western shore of the Hellespont, across which lay Asia proper (Arr. 1.11.3–5; Engels, 28–9).

The land route to Asia, at least initially, obviated the need to rely on the Greek navy for support. In the event, the vaunted Persian navy made no attempt to oppose the crossing of the Hellespont in early 334 BC. Either it was still tied down quelling the rebellion in Egypt or, more likely, realized that with a Macedonian bridgehead already established in the Troad by Parmenion's advance force, the fleet could not successfully interdict the crossing (Anson, 1989). Memnon's failure to eradicate the Macedonian advance force in the two years previous probably led the Persians to believe that the crossing could not be stopped and that Alexander would have to be met already mobilized in Asia. None the less, from the overall Persian point of view, the stability of the monarchy and the military situation in western Asia Minor had greatly improved from the early 330s BC when the situation was quite chaotic (Rahe [1980], 90; Ruzicka, 91). For the Persians, there was no

The alleged 'Tomb of Achilles' on the Scamandar plain outside of Troy. Alexander's visit to Troy was loaded with meaning in what could be seen as the latest chapter in the conflict between Greece and Asia.

reason for unnecessary panic. In fact, the local satraps and their military forces were already being mobilized in north-western Anatolia as the first line of defence against the invader.

The crossing into Asia

After Alexander reached Sestos, he left Parmenion to oversee the ferrying of the army to Abydos on Asian soil less than a mile across this narrow stretch of the Hellespont. Leaving the logistics of this operation to his deputy, Alexander took the opportunity to sojourn to Troy, a visit laden with deep symbolic significance. At Elaeus on the southern tip of the Chersonese, he sacrificed at the tomb of Protesilaus who was reputed to have been the first of the Greek soldiers to land in Asia during the Trojan War. Sailing across the strait towards the 'Achaean harbour', Alexander steered the ship himself and sacrificed a bull to Poseidon and the Nereids as well as pouring libations into the Hellespont in appeal for a safe crossing. Diodorus (17.17.2) even says that, upon landing, Alexander flung his spear towards Asia and leapt onto the shore before his comrades to signify 'that he had received Asia from the gods as a spear-won prize.' Further appropriate sacrifices and dedications were made at Troy itself, including Alexander's own armour which he exchanged for some left in the temple of Athena Ilias from the time of the Trojan War. The tombs of Achilles and other Homeric heroes were visited, venerated and sacrificed at, and the spirit of Trojan Priam appeased with a sacrifice as well.

These heady religious observations and honours were certainly called for in order to elicit divine support for an arduous and long military campaign, but they also provided a significant propaganda opportunity for Alexander. Like Homer's heroes of the epic *Illiad*, Alexander was leading 'Greeks' against their traditional enemies in Asia itself. Perhaps more important than the propitiatory acts themselves was the identification of Alexander's expedition as heir to Homer's tale. The new Achilles had, literally, landed.

Meanwhile, Parmenion was ferrying the bulk of the army across the Hellespont. That he was able to carry out this task with 160 triremes and

The enduring legacy of Homer. The poet as depicted on a 50 drachmes coin which was part of modern Greek coinage before the introduction of the Euro.

a great many cargo vessels (Arr. 1.11.6, cf. Justin (11.6.1) '182' ships) indicates that Alexander was able to muster a naval force of some size to cover the crossing against any possible Persian naval attack. The force numbers for Alexander's army are variously given in the ancient sources. Plutarch, in his work *On the Fortune or the Virtue of Alexander* (1.3.327d–e), quotes three sources contemporary with Alexander, two of whom, Aristobulus and Ptolemy, were also used by Arrian. Aristobulus said there were 30,000 infantry and 4,000 cavalry, while Ptolemy claimed there were 30,000 infantry and 5,000 cavalry. Providing higher figures, Anaximenes of Lampsacus, said there were 43,000 infantry and 5,500 cavalry. Arrian (1.11.3) must have used Ptolemy as his source when he says that the infantry was 'not much more than' 30,000, including the light-armed troops and archers, while the cavalry numbered 'more than' 5,000. A much later writer, Justin (11.6.2), gives similar figures of 32,000 infantry and 4,500 cavalry. These were the forces which Alexander took with him to the Hellespont. Additional forces numbering 12,000 infantry and 1,500 cavalry had been left under the command of Antipater in Macedonia (Diod. 17.17.5).

Diodorus also provides force numbers for the expeditionary force which he probably obtained from different sources and these are more detailed than those provided by Plutarch, Arrian and Justin. He states that the infantry was composed of 12,000 Macedonians, 7,000 allied

Replica of Greek cargo ship which sank off Cyprus c. 300 BC. Parmenion would have used similar vessels to ferry the army across the Hellespont and into Asia proper. (The Manchester Museum, The University of Manchester)

Macedonian and Allied force numbers at the crossing of the Hellespont					
	Arrian, 1.11.3	Diodorus, 17.17.3--5	Justin, 11.6.2	Plutarch, *Alex.* 15.2	Plutarch, *De Fort Alex.* 1.3.327d--e
Cavalry	'more than' 5,000		4,500	4,000–5,000	4,000 (Aristobulus) 5,000 (Ptolemy) 5,500 (Anaximenes)
Companions		1,800			
Thessalian		1,800			
Allied		600			
Thracian and Paeonian scouts		900			
Infantry	'not much more over' 30,000		32,000	30,000–43,000	30,000 (Aristobulus) 30,000 (Ptolemy) 43,000 (Anaximenes)
Macedonian		12,000			
Allied		7,000			
Mercenary		5,000			
Odyrsians, Triballians, Illyrians		7,000			
Archers and Agrianians		1,000			

Table of Macedonian and Allied force numbers at the crossing of the Granicus.

infantry, 5,000 mercenaries, 7,000 infantry from the Odyrsians, Triballians, and Illyrians, and 1,000 archers and Agrianians. This total of 32,000 infantry largely agrees with Plutarch, Arrian and Justin. Moreover, if Anaximenes' high figure of 43,000 infantry includes the 10,000 strong advance force sent in 336 BC and already present in the region, the figures essentially agree.

Unfortunately, Diodorus' numbers for the cavalry are not so straight-forward. He says there were 1,800 Macedonians, 1,800 Thessalian,

The walls of 'Troy VI' excavated by Heinrich Schliemann in the late 19th century. Alexander made a pilgrimage to Troy before rejoining the army outside of Abydos.

600 allied, and 900 Thracian and Paeonian scouts. Strangely, he continues to say that the total figure for the cavalry was 4,500 when, in fact, the figures he provides total 5,100. Much scholarly ink has been spilled trying to reconcile the various cavalry figures and many ingenious solutions have been proposed (e.g. Brunt, 32–6; Milns). Diodorus' actual total of 5,100 agrees quite closely with Arrian's 'more than' 5,000 and Arrian was using a contemporary source. This is also close to Ptolemy, whom Plutarch reports gave a cavalry figure of 5,000. In addition, as mentioned above, another contemporary source, Anaximenes of Lampsacus, provided a figure of 5,500 cavalry. This is the highest cavalry figure given and probably reflects the addition of cavalry

This detail from the Alexander Sarcophagus shows a Persian cavalryman who has just been killed, falling from his mount. Persian military strength traditionally lay in their horsemen. (akg-images/ Erich Lessing)

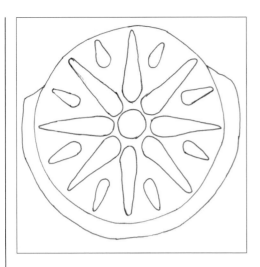

The traditional eight-pointed star emblem of Macedon. This drawing is based on the design of a miniature shield excavated from the tomb of Katerini in Macedon.

which was already operating with the advance force to the army brought from Macedonia. It is safe to conclude that the cavalry which was ferried across the Hellespont numbered in the vicinity of 5,000.

With the invasion army now in Asia and joined by the advance force, Alexander had roughly 40,000 infantry and 5,500 cavalry at his disposal. These marshalled at the plain of Arisbe and were joined by Alexander who had arrived from his visit to Troy. Now in Persian lands, Alexander sought to engage whatever force the Persians could muster against him as quickly as it could be brought to battle. The following day he departed eastwards into the Persian Empire. Clearly Alexander deemed it important to make a swift statement about his intent, ambitions and strength to Persians, Greeks, and Macedonians alike

The route to the Granicus River

Rather than set off south towards the Greek cities on the coast of western Asia Minor where the advance force had largely campaigned over the last two seasons, Alexander headed east around Mount Ida towards Dascylium, the capital of the Persian satrapy of Hellespontine Phrygia. Either he had intelligence, or (rightly) suspected that the satraps of the region would be collecting forces to oppose him in this location. The ancient sources also indicate that he now had provisions for only 30 days and that his treasury amounted to only 70 talents, while he owed 200 talents (Plut. *Alex.* 15.1). If he could engage and destroy whatever field army the local satraps would bring against him, he would both gain the resources of the region and secure his supply and communications line to Macedonia.

Before setting off, Alexander decided to leave behind the 7,000 Greek allied infantry and 5,000 mercenaries who had been brought over with the invasion force. Perhaps he suspected the loyalties of his Greek allies after the revolt of Thebes a year earlier. He probably assumed that since he was sure to face Greek mercenaries as the most significant part of the Persian infantry he would encounter, his own should be left behind. He would not test the loyalties of mercenaries brought over from Greece in this initial engagement. Moreover, this large force of allied and mercenary infantry would be a certain drain on his already dwindling supplies and, he may have thought, they could provide useful consolidation and garrison duties in and around the Hellespont and Troad, with the aim of later joining the Macedonian army when it returned.

In addition to these considerations, Alexander was to move swiftly, covering the roughly 60 miles from Arisbe to the Granicus in three days. For this sort of movement, he would only require his Macedonian infantry, the six 'brigades' (*taxeis*) of the *sarissa*-armed phalanx, and the hypaspists. These were all tough, veteran, and experienced campaigners. Although numbering only 12,000, Alexander could be confident that they would be more than a match for the infantry of the opposition, likely to be at best Greek hoplite mercenaries.

On the other hand, Alexander knew that Persian military strength, in number and quality, lay in their cavalry, and he therefore opted to take all of the cavalry available to him. The principal strike force of his army, the 1,800-strong Companion cavalry, and the 1,800 Thessalian cavalry were joined by the heavy cavalry of his Greek allies, which, numbering 600, was less of a potential concern regarding any questions of loyalty. The 900 light cavalry of *prodromoi*, Thracians and Paeonians were also part of the force. They were too useful to be left behind.

Leaving Arisbe, Alexander reached Percote and the following day came to the city of Lampsacus. There is a tale related by Pausanias, a Greek traveller who wrote in the 2nd century AD, that Anaximenes of Lampsacus tricked Alexander into sparing the city which the latter had decided to destroy because of its loyalty to the Persians. In fact, there is evidence that the city may have supported Memnon in 335 BC when he was fighting against the Macedonian advance force and had thereby incurred the wrath of Alexander (Bosworth [1980], 108). If so, Anaximenes may have done his fellow citizens an important office as Alexander bypassed the city without incident. At the end of the day's march the army encamped near the River Practicus, which may be identified with the River Paesus which empties into the Propontis (Sea of Marmara) at the northern end of the Hellespont.

The following day the army struck camp for Colonae and must have arrived at the town of Hermotus around midday. The exact route from Lampsacus to the Granicus is difficult to identify. Some maintain that near Lampsacus, Alexander turned inland, rejoining the River Practicus (on this theory, identified with the modern Umurbey Çay which flows into the Hellespont south of Lapeski) nearer its watershed in the uplands of the Ida Mountains (Foss, 497–8; Hammond [1980], 76). Unfortunately, Colonae and Hermotus, the only two place names mentioned regarding Alexander's route between Lampsacus and the River Granicus, have not been positively identified. Hermotus was probably located on the low foothills just south of the plain through which the Granicus flows and Colonae would have been farther west. If the conjectural location of Colonae is placed nearer the coast, then the coastal route, which is adopted in this text, is preferable to the inland route necessitated if the town is located farther south. Unless otherwise required, ancient armies generally followed coastal routes, and as Alexander made the journey in three (Arr. 1.12.6) or slightly more days (Diod. 17.18.1, 'a few days') it is likely that he avoided the mountainous region of the northern Ida uplands.

At some point after reaching Hermotus, Alexander dispatched a force under the command of one of the Companion cavalry, Panegorus, son of Lycagoras, to seize the coastal town of Priapus, which occupies a stretch of land roughly two miles north of where the Granicus empties into the Propontis. At Hermotus, Alexander was now just west of the River Granicus and from the hills would have been able to survey the plain surrounding the river in the distance.

Scouts (*skopoi*) were now sent forwards to reconnoitre the area. Alexander placed the scouts under the overall direction of Amyntas, son of Arrhabaeus, who led a squadron of Companion cavalry recruited from Apollonia in the Chalcidice. Amyntas' squadron commander (*ilarch*) was Socrates, son of Sathon and both of these men were to see important action in the opening stage of the battle. In addition to the scouts, four squadrons (*ilai*) of the *prodromoi* were sent in front of the army.

This depiction of a Bactrian (from ancient Bactria, now modern day north Afghanistan) comes from the eastern stairs in the Apadana ('reception hall') at Persepolis. Bactrian settlers in Asia Minor fought at the battle of the Granicus. (Jona Lendering, www.livius.org)

A detail of the reliefs on the stairways leading to the audience hall of Darius and Xerxes. A procession of Lydian tribute bearers led by ushers bring gifts from the outlying nations of the Persian empire. (Werner Forman Archive)

Persian movements

Although the Persians did not contest the crossing of Alexander's army into Asia they were no doubt aware that an invasion force had left the Macedonian heartland heading for Asia. Philip's earlier incursions with the advance force of Parmenion and Attalus would have alerted the Persians that there was aggressive intent from Macedonia. In early May the local satraps gathered in the region of Dascylium. Arsites, the satrap of Hellespontine Phrygia, the territory through which Alexander was now marching, was joined by satraps from the other Anatolian provinces. Arsames from Cilicia, the province north of Cyprus in the south-east of the peninsula, Atizyes, satrap of 'Greater' Phrygia in the interior of Anatolia, Mithrobuzanes, the satrap of southern Cappadocia, and Spithridates, the satrap of Lydia and Ionia, and his brother, Rhoesaces, gathered their forces in the fertile plain around Dascylium, roughly 50 miles east of the Granicus. These were joined by other Persian nobles, some of whom were relations of Darius, and the Greek mercenary commander Memnon, who had earlier received estates in the Troad from the Great King.

This fragment of pottery from the Acropolis of Athens (c. 530 BC) shows an oared warship carrying hoplites. Although heavily armed and on guard, they had to be careful not to shift position and unbalance the boat. (Athens, National Archaeological Museum, Nic Fields collection)

Alexander's movement east would have been a point of concern, but perhaps not unduly so. It is important to remember that in early 334 BC Alexander was very much an unknown quantity, and certainly not yet Alexander 'the Great' (Davis, 36). From intelligence, they would have been aware of his exploits, particularly since assuming the throne, but they had not had any direct contact with the Macedonian king, only 21 years of age at this point. The Great King himself, Darius III, felt no compulsion to rush to meet the young Macedonian. Over a thousand miles away in the heart of his empire he must have felt confident in the ability of his local commanders and their forces to stop the Macedonian incursion.

The forces which were marshalled by the satraps would have been raised locally. Around 5,000 Greek mercenaries were gathered to provide the infantry which the Persian satraps of Asia Minor regularly hired. Diodorus (17.19.4–5), the only source for the Persian order of battle, indicates that Arsames brought his own cavalry from Cilicia and that Memnon also commanded his own cavalry, presumably raised from his estates in the Troad. Arsites, in the battle order, commands cavalry from Paphlagonia, the region on the southern coast of the Black Sea. Cavalry from Media, Bactria, and Hyrcania are also listed as present, which may appear anomalous as these provinces are from the central and eastern parts of the Persian Empire. However, there is no need to believe that these were brought to the region specifically to face Alexander. Rather, they would have been raised locally from colonists of these regions who had long ago settled in Asia Minor in return for their services to the Great King in this area (Lane Fox, 119). Cavalry was traditionally the strongest arm of any Persian military force, and it is likely that more than 10,000 were assembled by the satraps.

The fertile plain around Dascylium would have meant this western Persian field army was well provisioned. In addition, the town lay on an important crossroads in the region. The road south led to the chief city of Lydia, Sardis, and access to the large cities on the western Anatolian

An image of *Olympias*, a full-scale reconstruction of an Athenian trireme, which shows the hot and narrow space below the decks called the Thrantitai station. Although the oarsmen at least had some fresh air, with the open-sided outrigger it was a dangerous place to be. (Nic Fields collection)

seaboard farther south such as Ephesus and Miletus. In fact, Sardis was the western terminus of the famous Persian Royal Road which led eastwards to the capital Susa. North of Dascylium lay the important coastal city of Cyzicus, which remained autonomous and supportive of the Macedonians. A 2nd century AD complier of military stratagems says that in 335 BC Memnon had tried to trick his way into Cyzicus by dressing his men as Macedonians. The Cyzicenes, thinking the approaching force was Alexander's commander in the region, Calas, almost opened the gates but spotted the ruse at the last minute. Memnon had to settle for ravaging the land outside the city (Polyaenus, *Stratagems of War* 5.44).

As the interior of the Troad region is dominated by the Ida mountain range, roads eastwards from the Hellespont took a north-easterly direction and descended into the plain of Adrasteia through which the River Granicus flows. As Alexander was approaching from this direction, the Persian army and its commanders set out from Dascylium to the town of Zeleia (modern Sariköy) approximately 20 miles east of the Granicus.

The war council at Zeleia

The Persian force apparently reached Zeleia by late May and it was here that Alexander's crossing into Asia was probably reported to the commanders. There is a fascinating insight into Persian strategic thinking at this point, and into the command structure of this Persian army, thanks to a report preserved in Arrian (1.12.8–10) and Diodorus (17.18.2–4) of a war council that was held amongst the Persian satraps and Memnon very shortly before, perhaps even on the eve of, the battle.

The bow of *Olympias*, showing the bronze-sheathed ram, the weapon of destruction on which Greek naval power was based. Just before the moment of impact, the bo'sun would order the oarsmen to switch to backing water, in order to keep the ram from penetrating too far. (Nic Fields collection)

The mercenary commander from Rhodes, Memnon, initially suggested that the best course of action was not to engage Alexander immediately because the Macedonians were 'far superior' in infantry and had their own commander leading them, while Darius was not present to lead his army. Rather, Memnon counselled, the Persians should withdraw, destroying the fodder and provisions in the area, burning the growing crops, and even destroying the towns and cities of the region. This 'scorched-earth' policy would deprive Alexander of the supplies he would require (Engels, 30), and it is perhaps tempting to wonder whether Memnon had intelligence that Alexander's army was already reduced to a month's supply of provisions, a claim made in Plutarch (*Alex.* 15.1).

Diodorus adds the additional comment that Memnon also advocated sending land and naval forces across to mainland Europe in lieu of immediate engagement in Asia, in effect opening up a diversionary second front. It is doubtful that this grandiose plan was actually mooted before the battle of the Granicus although it may have been more seriously considered throughout the latter half of 334 BC and in 333 BC before Memnon, the one man who might lead such an expedition, died of illness.

Olympias in dry-dock, showing the three banks of oars from which the name trireme is derived. The trireme was the standard warship of the ancient Mediterranean.

Though perhaps operationally valid, Memnon's proposal required a considerable sacrifice on the part of those satraps whose territories he was effectively arguing should be surrendered without a fight in the interests of the greater strategic objective. Arsites, the satrap of Hellespontine Phrygia whose province would be the first to suffer under Memnon's 'scorched-earth' policy, flatly refused to allow 'a single house' of his subjects to be destroyed. The obligation of a satrap was to protect the lands which had been conferred upon him by the Great King and, although it is ultimately dubious how truly 'his own' were the 'subjects' of the region, simply abandoning his satrapy to the enemy could surely be interpreted as a violation of his duties as a Persian noble. Moreover, as Diodorus states (17.18.3), Memnon's advice probably struck at the 'dignity' and code of honour held by this (or, indeed, any other) aristocracy.

Arsites' fellow satraps were in agreement with their colleague and Memnon's counsel was rejected. Memnon's suggestion was apparently so outrageous that they even began to distrust his motives. Arrian (1.12.10) says that the satraps suspected 'Memnon of deliberately attempting to delay the fight for the sake of honour he might gain from the Great King'. Memnon's position depended directly upon the favour of the Great King, rather than the satraps of Asia Minor, and they may have regarded his situation with some jealousy. It has been suggested that Arsites, as the satrap of Hellespontine Phrygia, had particular reason to mistrust Memnon who held territories within Arsites' own satrapy (McCoy, 428–9). Despite Memnon's earlier services to the Persian throne, why should the local satraps defer to a Greek, and a *condottiere*, at the expense of their own authority? On the other hand, it may be the case that the extant authors took the story of this council from earlier writers who desired to make a Greek, Memnon, appear more sagacious (as is always the case with hindsight) than his Persian counterparts.

Painted tiles from a frieze from Susa depicting archers. Taken from the Palace of Darius and dating from between 522 and 586 BC. (Ancient Art and Architecture Collection)

Although it has been suggested that Darius had made early preparations for the Macedonian invasion (Garvin, 98) the fact that there was a war council at Zeleia implies that the local satraps had not received explicitly direct instructions from the Great King regarding the conduct of the war. The nature of this war council raises the interesting question of the Persian command structure at the battle of the Granicus. It has been argued that part of the reason for the Persian failure at the Granicus was that the Persians conducted a battle by committee (Davis, 44; Badian [2000], 255). However, it may have been the case that Arsites held a position closer to supreme command, possibly as some sort of *primus inter pares* among the nobles (Briant, 820–3; Badian [1977], 283). It was his territory where any engagement with Alexander would first be met; he also takes the lead in rejecting, on behalf of the satraps, Memnon's advice; and perhaps most tellingly, he survives the battle but later commits suicide (Arr. 1.16.3) implying a responsibility and, indeed, culpability greater than those of the other Persian nobility who survived.

BATTLE

TERRAIN AND TOPOGRAPHY

I n addition to the ancient authors, the other crucial source of information we have about the battle of the Granicus is the current terrain and topography of the battlefield. The identification of the ancient River Granicus has never been in any doubt as the ancient geographer Strabo, who wrote a 17-book work known as the *Geographia* in the late 1st/early 2nd century AD, located the Granicus between Priapus in the west and the River Aesepus (modern Gönen Çay) in the east (Strabo, *Geog.* 587). Only one river of any significance lies between these two points, the modern Biga Çay, which flows north from the Ida mountain range through the modern town of Biga into the Sea of Marmara via the plain known in antiquity as Adrasteia. In addition, there is no reason to believe that the river has substantially changed its course since the battle was fought some 2,300 years ago (Foss, 500-1; Harl, 304).

The extensive plain around the river is largely flat and featureless. To the west, in the direction of Hermotus from where Alexander approached, there are low lying foothills which, for the most part, gradually descend to the valley plain. To the south there are larger hills broken by the valleys formed by the Biga Çay and its tributaries flowing from the foothills of the Ida uplands. To the east, the plain, interrupted only by some low hills to the south-east, extends along the coast of the Sea of Marmora.

View to the north of the plain of 'Adrasteia' from the village of Adiye. The River 'Granicus' is marked by the tree line in the middle distance. It is doubtful that the course of the river has changed since antiquity.

A low rise of hills about 100 metres in height lays roughly two-and-a-half miles east of the river. Much further beyond (to the centre and right of the photo) runs another range of much higher hills.

In the immediate vicinity of the battlefield, there was an ancient lake, the Ece Göl (now drained and used for cattle grazing), west of the river near where the battle occurred. South of the lake near the river lay some small broken hills, rarely reaching more than 50 metres in height. To the north-east of the lake the plain is flat and devoid of significant topography or vegetation. Approximately 2.5 miles east of the river is a ridge of low hills attaining a height of approximately 100 metres, but the plain between these hills and the river is again flat and today heavily cultivated.

The outstanding topographical feature of the plain is the river itself, both today and in antiquity. Until very recent earthworks to uniformly embank the 'Granicus', the river ran, in late May, in a small channel through a broad flat riverbed of exposed gravel and fine sand. The river itself is quite shallow in spring and was completely fordable without much difficulty in every place as the water-line seldom rose above a horse's knee and the flow was gentle. The banks which line both sides of the riverbed occasionally rose quite steeply but were generally broken in many places by gradually sloping gravel banks allowing access to the plains on either side which gently slope away to the west and east. Small trees and shrubs were present on the river banks in small numbers and, although not of a high enough density to impede entrance or exit of the riverbed, these may have made it difficult to climb up some sections of the banks.

In a conversation before the battle, Parmenion is said to have advised Alexander to delay the battle until the next day because the river was 'deep' in parts and the banks 'very high' and 'cliff like' (Arr. 1.13.4). Parmenion argued that they should encamp for the night and, since the Persians were inferior in infantry and thus unlikely to remain encamped nearby, the Macedonians could ford the river unopposed in the morning. Elsewhere, the Macedonian officers are described as worried about 'the depth of the river, and of the roughness and unevenness of the farther banks' (Plut. *Alex.* 16.1). Plutarch further stated (*Alex.* 16.3) that during the battle the flow of the river was strong enough to sweep men off their feet.

The southern section of the river Granicus as it appears today. This photograph was taken from the bridge at the village of Çinarköprü. Alexander and the Companion cavalry engaged the Persians near here.

However, these descriptions of the river as a raging, cavernous torrent should be dismissed as artistic licence on the part of the ancient authors which serve, unnecessarily, to heroicize Alexander's decision to cross the river and fight the battle on that afternoon. Of course, the river and more particularly the banks were an obstacle. The banks were steep and high *in places*, and did afford, again *in places*, a higher ground from which the Persian cavalry enjoyed some defensive advantage, but the river in itself was not an insurmountable obstacle. Once the strategic decision had been made to meet Alexander in the plain of Adrasteia, the Persians naturally chose to make their stand at the River Granicus as it provided the only defensive advantage in an otherwise flat, featureless plain. The river and the banks would necessarily slow and, potentially, disperse any attack by cavalry, and even more so infantry. It could even provide some high ground advantageous to the discharge of spears but, at least to Alexander, it was not sufficient an impediment to prevent an immediate attack. Alexander dismissed Parmenion's suggestion to delay the attack as lightly as he dismissed the river itself, which Alexander, somewhat more correctly than his officers, contemptuously described as a 'little stream' (Arr. 1.13.6). He also remarked that the 'Hellespont would blush in shame' if Alexander were to be afraid of crossing the Granicus (Plut. *Alex.* 14.2, cf. Arr. 1.13.6).

PRELIMINARIES TO THE BATTLE

In approaching the river, Alexander had marched his army in a 'double' (*diplçn*) phalanx formation with two phalanxes of infantry flanked by cavalry on either side and screened by light infantry and scouts in the front. When the scouts reported that the Persians were occupying the far bank of the river, Alexander was quickly able to arrange the army in battle formation. The leftmost position was taken by the 1,800-strong Thessalian cavalry under the command of Calas, who had been one of the commanders sent with the advance force in 335 BC. To the right of

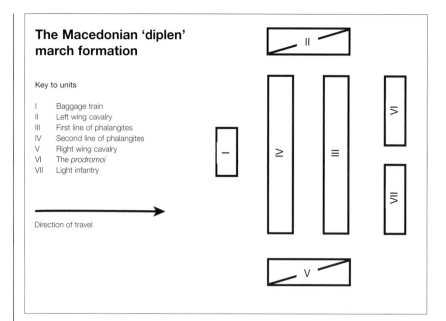

The Macedonian 'diplen' march formation

Key to units

I	Baggage train
II	Left wing cavalry
III	First line of phalangites
IV	Second line of phalangites
V	Right wing cavalry
VI	The *prodromoi*
VII	Light infantry

Direction of travel

Diagram of the Macedonian *diplçn* march formation. The meaning of this term in Arrian is unclear and earlier scholars depict the infantry deployed in columnar formation. However, it is likely that the phalanx was assembled into two linear formations which would facilitate swift deployment for battle.

these were placed the allied Greek cavalry under Philip, son of Menelaus, and the Thracian cavalry from Odrysia under Agathon respectively. The 2,700-strong cavalry of the left wing were under the overall command of Parmenion. In the centre were placed the six *taxeis* ('brigades') of the *sarissa*-wielding *pezetairoi*. The commanders of each 1,500 strong *taxis* ('brigade') were: Meleager, Philip son of Amyntas, Amyntas, Craterus, Coenus, and Perdiccas. To the right of the phalanx were the 3,000-strong *hypaspists*. On the right wing, and under the overall command of Alexander, were the 1,800-strong Companion cavalry under Philotas, son of Parmenion with the *prodromoi* and Paeonian cavalry to their left and the archers and Agrianian javelinmen screening in front. With the phalanx in the centre drawn up to a depth of eight men, the Macedonian line extended approximately 2.5 miles from the confluence of the river where Alexander and the Companion cavalry were stationed on the right wing northwards towards the cavalry under Parmenion on the left wing.

A rough Persian order of battle is given in Diodorus (17.19.4) which states that Memnon of Rhodes was stationed on the left wing with Arsames 'each with their own cavalry'. Interestingly, Memnon was not in command of the Greek mercenaries who were positioned behind the full line of Persian cavalry and apparently were under the command of a Persian named Omares (Arr. 1.16.3, Bosworth [1980], 125). To the right of Memnon and Arsamenes was Arsites, leading the cavalry from Paphlagonia, and then the Hyrcanian cavalry under Spithridates. Other cavalry of unspecified nationality occupied the centre and to their right were the Bactrian cavalry. On the right wing was a cavalry contingent under Rheomithres with the rightmost position taken by the cavalry from Media. The contingents are variously reported at strengths of one or two thousand and the total cavalry force likely numbered more than 10,000, or roughly twice the number of Alexander's cavalry (cf. Diod 17.19.4). The number of Greek mercenaries was around 5,000, significantly fewer than the 12,000-strong Macedonian phalanx.

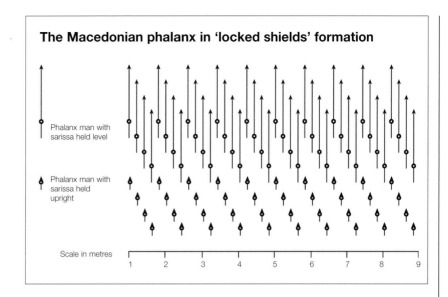

The Macedonian phalanx in 'locked shields' formation

Phalanx man with
sarissa held level

Phalanx man with
sarissa held
upright

Scale in metres

1 2 3 4 5 6 7 8 9

The decision by the Persians to position their cavalry at or near the river and place the infantry behind has been criticized as a serious tactical error, but the practice was not unknown to the Persians. In 401 BC local Persian forces attempted to block the passage into Armenia of the '10,000' Greek mercenaries who were attempting to return home out of the heart of the Persian Empire after the death of their paymaster Cyrus in his failed attempt to usurp the Persian throne. As the Greek commander Xenophon recounts, the Persians lined cavalry across the Centrites river and placed infantry on the rising ground behind (Xenophon *Anabasis* 4.3.3). Similarly, at the Granicus, given their inferiority in infantry, it would have made little sense for the Persians to have placed their Greek mercenaries directly opposite the Macedonian phalanx because the mercenaries would not have been able to match the length of the Macedonian line without being spread hopelessly thin.

As noted above, after the two armies had been arrayed, Arrian (1.13.3–7) reports a conversation where Parmenion advises that the battle be delayed until the following morning. This advice is strongly rejected by Alexander, but the ultimate source of this story must also have been known to Diodorus because he writes as if Alexander accepted Parmenion's advice; encamped that night, crossed the river at dawn and deployed his forces before the Persians could stop him (Diod. 17.19.3). The irreconcilable accounts of Diodorus and Arrian in this regard have caused difficulties for later historians reconstructing the course of events, with a minority accepting Diodorus' view of a postponed engagement (Lane Fox, 121–2, cf. Green's revision in his 1991 addition, 172–7 and 489–512). However, Plutarch (*Alex.* 16.2) was of the opinion that Alexander attacked immediately, impetuously disregarding the reservations of his officers, a view which is in accord with Arrian's depiction of events. It is highly unlikely that Alexander would have delayed his attack once he had brought the Persians to battle. In addition, it is even more unlikely that the Persians, having sought what protection and advantage the River Granicus could afford, would allow or somehow be caught unawares whilst Alexander's entire army crossed the river and deployed for battle the following morning.

The view adopted in this book is that Diodorus' account is confused, perhaps because he thought that Parmenion's suggestion was actually accepted by Alexander, and should be disregarded (Badian [1977], 272–4, Hammond [1980] 74–6, Davis, 40–2).

With both armies nervously lined up on opposite banks of the riverbed, Alexander made himself conspicuous by his appearance and entourage (Arr. 1.14.4). His helmet fixed with two large white plumes would have clearly marked him out to the Persians on the far bank and certainly to Memnon, Arsames, and Arsites directly opposite. The other satraps may have noticed this as well as in the course of events many of them appear in battle with or near the king himself. In fact, the disposition of Memnon and Arsites in particular may indicate that the immediate Persian tactical objective was to kill the young king himself (Badian [2000], 255). Attacking the head of an army was a typical Persian tactic, and in this case particularly apt. At the battle of Cunaxa in 401 BC, the Persian satrap and failed usurper, Cyrus, ordered his Greek mercenary commander, Clearchus, to attack the Persian Great King directly, stating, 'if we are victorious there, our whole task is accomplished.' (Xenophon *Anabasis* 1.8.12) Perhaps by placing the cavalry in front of their mercenary infantry, contrary to received wisdom and normal practice, they intended to reach Alexander himself as soon as was possible, in the belief that killing the young Macedonian king would end the war at its inception.

The initial attack

While Alexander's movements were being marked by the Persians, there was a significant lapse in time, during which the armies, deployed and ready for battle, observed each other in silence (Arr. 1.14.5). It was perhaps during this lull that the satraps leading other cavalry contingents gravitated towards Alexander's position at the southern end of the river near its confluence with a branching tributary. The Persians were waiting for the Macedonians to enter the river where the attack would be slowed and the possibility of counterattacks could break up any forward momentum.

Alexander then ordered Amyntas, son of Arrhabaeus, to lead a vanguard force into the river. The *prodromoi*, the Paeonian cavalry and the contingent of Agrianian javelinmen descended into the river bed along with an *ile* of the Companion cavalry led by Socrates. The Persian reaction was swift and severe as they began to rain down javelins from their bank while some of the cavalry also descended into the riverbed to obstruct the access points out of the river. Clearly, the Persians were intent on attacking the Macedonians while the latter had to navigate the river channel itself, both from the high ground with missile fire and at the edge of those points where the sloping gravel inclines allowed easier

The area to the west of the River Granicus. The (now drained) march of Ece Gol is visible in the middle right distance. Alexander and his army would have bypassed this to the north in their approach to the river.

egress onto the far bank. The ancient sources note that in the course of the action the footing became difficult and slippery for the attackers, which further hindered the attack (Arr. 1.15.2, Plut. *Alex.* 16.3).

The advance force began to take serious casualties with Socrates' 200-strong *ile* of the Companion cavalry losing 25 men in the fighting. Although fighting bravely and staunchly, the advance force was now engaged with some of the strongest Persian cavalry led by Memnon and his sons. In addition, they were becoming seriously outnumbered as further Persian cavalry began to reinforce the counterattack. Some portions of the advance force were being forced back in retreat to the Macedonian lines when the sounds of trumpets and the Macedonian war cry were raised throughout the Macedonian right wing (Arr. 1.14.7).

Alexander's advance force had not succeeded in gaining the far bank, but they had not been sent on a suicide mission by an uncaring commander. This 'pawn-sacrifice', as it has been called (Devine, 1988), had drawn some, and increasingly more, of the Persian cavalry off the banks on the far side, engaged Memnon in the initial fighting, and increasingly disrupted the orderliness of the Persian defence as units and their commanders pushed towards the initial area of contact. More than simply a feint, the advance force had, in contemporary terms, begun to 'shape the battlefield' in Alexander's favour (Gaebel, 179).

The main cavalry engagement

Alexander now committed himself and the full weight of the Companion cavalry, the most potent force in his army, against the Persian left wing. Having descended into the river bed, Alexander led the formation obliquely to the right of the units in Amyntas' advance force which where engaged in heavy combat in and around the river channel, some of whom were in disarrayed retreat or were being pushed back. One ancient author states that Alexander attempted to outflank

A Persian cavalryman run through by Alexander's lance (*xyston*). From a line drawing of Alexander mosaic.

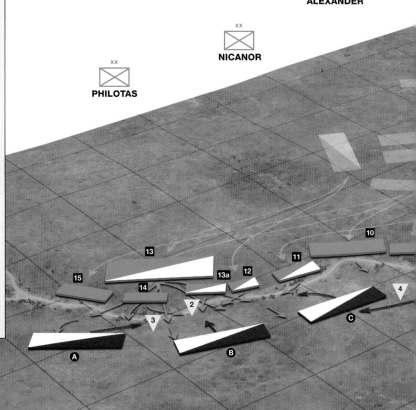

MACEDONIAN AND ALLIES

Listed from their left wing.
[Force numbers are in square brackets.]

Left Wing
1   Thessalian cavalry [1,800] (Parmenion)
2   Allied Greek cavalry [600] (Calas)
3   Thracian Odrysian cavalry [300] (Agathon)

Centre
4   Foot companion taxis (i.e. 'brigade')
     [1,500] (Meleager)
5   Foot companion taxis [1,500] (Philip)
6   Foot companion taxis [1,500] (Amyntas)
7   Foot companion taxis [1,500] (Craterus)
8   Foot companion taxis [1,500] (Coenus)
9   Foot companion taxis [1,500] (Perdiccas)
10 Hypaspists (i.e. infantry armed more like
     traditional Greek hoplites) [3,000] (Nicanor)

Right Wing (Alexander)
11 Prodromoi (i.e. light cavalry, scouts) [300]
     (no known commander)
12 Paeonian cavalry [300]
     (no known commander)
13a Socrates' ilï (i.e. 'squadron') of Companion
     cavalry [200] (Socrates)
13 Companion cavalry [1,800 inclusive of
     Socrates' ilï] (Philotas)
14 Agrianian javelinmen [500] (Amyntas as
     overall commander of the 'advance force'
     of prodromoi, Paeonian cavalry, Socrates'
     ilï and probably the Agrianians)
15 Cretan archers [500]
     (no known commander)

▼ EVENTS

1. Alexander arrives at the low ridge of hills which overlook the Granicus from the west. The army is in march formation with two lines of the phalangites protected on either wing by cavalry. The army is screened by the prodromoi (scouts) and light infantry. The baggage train follows in the rear

2. The initial attack led by Socrates' ilï of Companion cavalry, the prodromoi, Paeonian cavalry, and a 'unit' of infantry (most likely the Agrianians). This advance force attacks into the river and towards the far bank. It draws some units of the Persian cavalry into the riverbed and away from their advantageous positions on and near the riverbanks.

3. Alexander and the Companion cavalry engage those Persian cavalry in the riverbed and river. Alexander himself fights in heavy close combat with the satraps who have rushed against him. Ascending accessible exit points on the far bank, the Macedonians and Alexander begin to engage Persian cavalry on the plain beyond the far bank.

4. Mithridates and other satraps attempt to lead a counterattack to stem the tide of Macedonian cavalry now sweeping up the banks and onto the plain. Mithridates is killed by Alexander.

5. The phalanx begins to move across the river.

6. Parmenion and the left wing cavalry attack across the river.

PHASE I – THE CAVALRY ENGAGEMENT

Attack of Alexander the Great's Macedonian and Greek allies across the River Granicus. The two armies meet at the river and array for battle in the afternoon of a late May day in 334 BC.

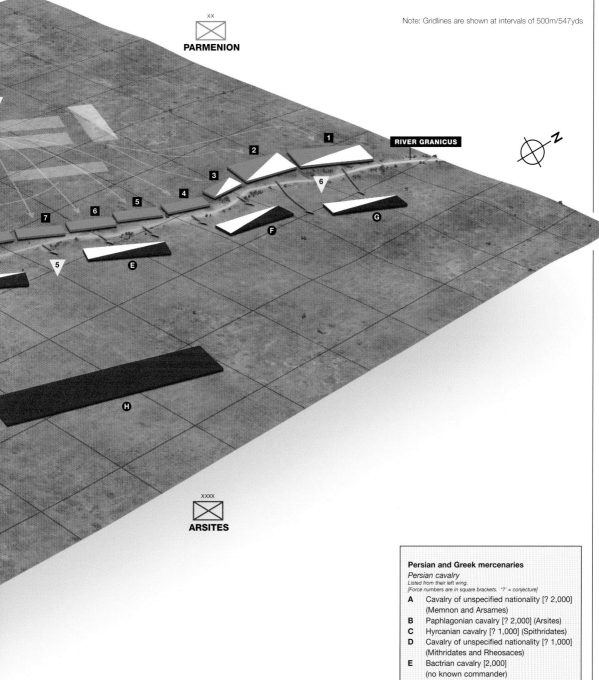

Note: Gridlines are shown at intervals of 500m/547yds

PARMENION

xx

RIVER GRANICUS

ARSITES

xxxx

Persian and Greek mercenaries

Persian cavalry
Listed from their left wing.
[Force numbers are in square brackets. '?' = conjecture]

A Cavalry of unspecified nationality [? 2,000] (Memnon and Arsames)

B Paphlagonian cavalry [? 2,000] (Arsites)

C Hyrcanian cavalry [? 1,000] (Spithridates)

D Cavalry of unspecified nationality [? 1,000] (Mithridates and Rheosaces)

E Bactrian cavalry [2,000] (no known commander)

F Cavalry of unspecified nationality [2,000] (Rheomithres)

G Median cavalry [1,000] (no known commander)

Greek mercenaries
Behind Persian cavalry

H Greek mercenaries (Omares)

63

the Persian left by attacking 'upstream waterwards' (Polyaenus, *Stratagems of War* 4.3.16) but it is more likely that Alexander was simply leading the bulk of the Companion cavalry to the right, i.e. 'upstream', to avoid clashing with the units of the advance force. His decision to use the confluence of the Granicus with a tributary of the river just to the south of his deployment as protection against his own right wing being outflanked precluded, in turn, the sort of broad sweeping manoeuvre implied by Polyaenus. Not only was the direction of attack initially oblique in direction but according to Arrian the formation was echeloned in order to reach the far bank in a line and not be caught in columns (Arr. 1.14.7). This fanning out of the Companion cavalry allowed them to approach the far bank as a more or less solid line, since those *ilai* on the left would have slowed as they approached the mêlée involving the advance force and the Persian cavalry. If the bulk of Persian cavalry in the vicinity was moving directly towards the initial point of attack, the Companion cavalry, last to extend rightwards, may have met less opposition during the crossing of the riverbed and channel as they drove for their access points out of the river.

Alexander, leading the charge of the Companion cavalry, made first contact with the enemy right of the point where the initial attack had been blunted. Here the Persian cavalry were now massed and Arrian (1.15.3) comments that the 'leaders themselves were posted' here as well. Diodorus (17.20.2–3) is more specific when he states that,

The satrap of Ionia, Spithridates, a Persian by birth and son-in-law of King Darius, a man of superior courage, hurled himself at the Macedonian lines with a large body of cavalry, and with an array of forty companions, all Royal Relatives [i.e. an honorific title of high nobility] of outstanding valour, pressed hard on the opposite line and in a fierce attack slew some of his opponents and wounded others. As the force of this attack seemed dangerous, Alexander turned his horse toward the satrap and rode at him.

The cavalry of both sides were now fully committed in and around the river with the Macedonians struggling to force ways up the far bank. The

The riverbed of the Granicus river at present. In summer the river itself runs in small channels and much of the fine sand and gravel of the riverbed is exposed between the two banks. Alexander's 'near miss' probably occurred in the riverbed.

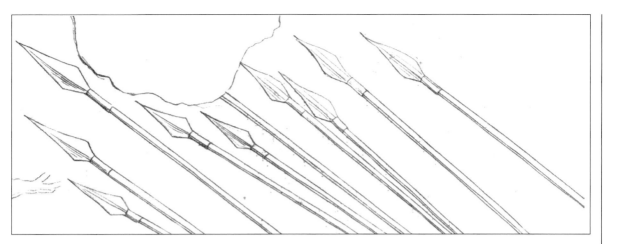

Detail of Macedonian *sarissae* from a line drawing of the Alexander Mosaic. Opposed only by javelins thrown from the Persian cavalry on the far bank the Macedonian cavalry slowly crossed the river and gained the far bank.

two sides had now become so enmeshed that, 'though they fought on horseback, it seemed more like an infantry than a cavalry battle' (Arr. 1.15.4). Amidst the confusion of the intense close combat the discipline and strength of the Macedonian Companion cavalry began to tell. Although the short sword and even shoulder-barging must have been used to good effect in the heated mêlée (Gabel, 162–3, 167), Arrian (1.15.5) ascribed the turning point to the Macedonians' efficient use of the cornel-wood cavalry *xyston* (lance) which was used to strike at the face of both horse and rider (Arr. 1.16.1). Thrusting at the face was the most effective use of a lance against a horse at it caused the animal to rear up and greatly increased the chances of it unseating its rider who, in this case, did not have the benefit of stirrups. If the lance was used to strike the horse's chest or body the force required for a fatal blow was likely to cause the *xyston* to fracture and break, which was a common occurrence, and a horse not killed in this manner was likely to lash out at the goading (Devine [1986], 275).

Alexander's 'near miss'

In amongst these individual battles, the Persian satraps made for Alexander himself. All three ancient sources relate that Alexander was involved in a fierce struggle which very nearly cost him his life. Unfortunately, they do not agree with regard to the participants involved or the precise sequence of events. In Diodorus' version, Spithridates hurls a javelin which pierces Alexander's breastplate. Alexander, in turn, is able to shake off the weapon and drive his *xyston* into the chest of the satrap. However, the blow is not fatal as the *xyston* snaps and, with sword drawn, Spithridates is only finally overcome when Alexander thrusts the shaft of his lance into the satrap's face. As this is unfolding, the satrap Rhoesaces rides up and strikes Alexander on the helmet with his sword, splitting the helmet but causing only a slight head wound. As Rhoesaces is poised to deliver the fatal blow, 'Black' Cleitus rides up and hacks off the Persian's arm (Diod. 17.20.3–7).

In Arrian's account of the incident, it is Mithridates who is initially dispatched by Alexander while Rhoesaces strikes Alexander on the helmet. Alexander is able to recover and drive his lance through his attacker, killing him. As this is happening, 'Black' Cleitus lops off the arm of Spithridates, who is set to deliver the *coup de grace* to the

65

ALEXANDER'S LIFE SAVED BY 'BLACK' CLEITUS DURING FIGHTING IN THE RIVER GRANICUS (pages 66–67)

On a clear late afternoon [1] in May 334 BC Alexander brought his army into action against the Persians for the first time at the river Granicus. After the battle lines had been arrayed, the ancient historian Plutarch (*Alex.* 16.7) says that Alexander made himself conspicuous by his actions and appearance, particularly with his 'helmet's crest, on either side of which was fixed a plume of wonderful size and whiteness' [2].

The battle was initiated when a detachment of the cavalry, the *prodromoi* and Paeonian cavalry, under Amyntas, accompanied by the Agrianian javelin men, entered the riverbed and moved towards the Persian cavalry marshalled on the far bank. They were joined by a squadron (*ile*) of the Companion cavalry commanded by Socrates, son of Sathon, who were intended to make first contact with the enemy. Socrates' *ile* did in fact suffer heavy casualties when met by the initial resistance of the Persian cavalry who hurled javelins from the often elevated positions of the far bank and riverbed. Alexander now committed the bulk of the Companion cavalry. The Companion cavalryman on the right of the scene is without the linen cuirass typically worn but wears the distinctive Boeotian style cavalry helmet and brandishes the straight sword for use in close combat [3]. In the river the Macedonians were met by the Persian cavalry under the command of several satraps, whose eagerness to enter the fray suggests they hoped to kill Alexander himself and end the Macedonian invasion before it had a chance to begin. The Persian cavalry fought with spears (*palta*) designed for throwing as well as stabbing and wore a very distinctive felt headgear which covered the neck and head, and linen corselets which covered their colourful full length trousers and long-sleeved tunics [4].

The fighting in the river was intense and close-order, with, according to the ancient historian Arrian (1.15.4), the cavalry of both sides fighting 'more like infantry', largely because they were impeded by the water in the river channel and the large numbers of cavalry gravitating toward the action at the point of the initial attack. In the midst of this struggle, the ancient sources relate that Alexander was set upon by the satraps Mithridates, Rhoesaces, and Spithridates. The accounts of the historians are not entirely consistent, but the main elements reconstructed in this scene are largely based on Arrian's version of events (1.15.6-8).

After grappling with and striking down the Persian satrap Mithridates, Alexander is struck on the helmet by another satrap, Rhoesaces, whom he is none the less able to kill with his lance which shatters in the process [5]. However, Rhoesaces' blow has cracked Alexander's helmet and Alexander is left dazed and momentarily vulnerable. Another satrap, Spithridates, raises his arm holding the curved Persian 'kopis' sword to deliver the *coup-de-grace* against the Macedonian king [6]. At the last moment, the upraised limb is severed from Spithridates' body by 'Black' Cleitus, commander (*iliarch*) of the 'Royal squadron' (*agema*) of the Companion cavalry, thereby saving Alexander's life [7].

Ultimately, the Persian cavalry were forced back by the weight of the Companion cavalry, largely due to the effectiveness and reach of the Macedonian cavalry lance [8]. With the entrance of the infantry phalanx into the battle, the Persian centre collapsed, followed by the wings as the Persian cavalry fled the battlefield.

otherwise occupied Alexander (Arr. 1.15.7–8). Finally, in Plutarch's description of the event, Alexander is pierced by a javelin and then set upon by Rhoesaces and Spithridates, the latter of whom is struck by Alexander's lance. Spithridates then strikes and splits Alexander's helmet but before he can strike again he is driven through with a lance by 'Black' Cleitus, while Alexander simultaneously runs through Rhoesaces with a sword (Plut. *Alex.* 16.4–5).

Although it is impossible to reconcile the details of the event as related in these accounts, they do agree on three common points. First, the Persian satraps made a concerted and determined attack on Alexander himself. Apparently, killing the Macedonian king was the main, and perhaps only, tactical objective from their perspective. In this, they very nearly succeeded because – second – all the accounts agree that Alexander was struck on the head and that it was likely that the conspicuous helmet, which he had donned for the battle and which so clearly marked him out, had saved his life from the initial blow. Thirdly, his life was ultimately preserved by the Companion cavalryman, 'Black' Cleitus, who, fortuitously, was able to eliminate the attacker when Alexander was at his most vulnerable and at the last moment before the death blow was to be delivered.

There is no reason to believe that this event was a literary creation designed to heroicise the king because, although the *mano-a-mano* combat is spectacularly dramatic, it is not Alexander but 'Black' Cleitus who appears most 'heroic'. Rather it is more plausible, particularly as the three accounts agree in their fundamentals, that Arrian, Plutarch, and Diodorus had taken this story from an author (or authors) who had composed this history much nearer to Alexander's own lifetime. If this is so, then that source (or sources) was not in a position to either invent what was clearly a central moment in the battle since if the source of this event wrote during Alexander's lifetime or shortly thereafter, i.e. within the lifetimes of those who fought with and knew Alexander, he could not, without appearing as a liar, have invented a story about the king which was known to be false and, moreover, was not particularly flattering to him. On the other hand, it is also unlikely that a contemporary, or near-contemporary, author would

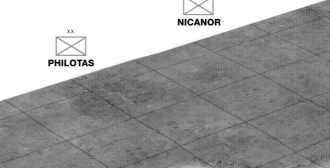

MACEDONIAN AND ALLIES

Listed from their left wing.
[Force numbers are in square brackets.]

Left Wing

1 Thessalian cavalry [1,800] (Parmenion)
2 Allied Greek cavalry [600] (Calas)
3 Thracian Odrysian cavalry [300] (Agathon)

Centre

4 Foot companion taxis (i.e. 'brigade')
   [1,500] (Meleager)
5 Foot companion taxis [1,500] (Philip)
6 Foot companion taxis [1,500] (Amyntas)
7 Foot companion taxis [1,500] (Craterus)
8 Foot companion taxis [1,500] (Coenus)
9 Foot companion taxis [1,500] (Perdiccas)
10 Hypaspists (i.e. infantry armed more like
   traditional Greek hoplites) [3,000] (Nicanor)

Right Wing (Alexander)

11 Prodromoi (i.e. light cavalry, scouts) [300]
   (no known commander)
12 Paeonian cavalry [300]
   (no known commander)
13 Companion cavalry [1,800 inclusive of
   Socrates' ilî] (Philotas)
14 Agrianian javelinmen [500] (Amyntas)
15 Cretan archers [500]
   (no known commander)

ALEXANDER

NICANOR

PHILOTAS

▼ EVENTS

1. **The Persian cavalry on the left wing flee after they are unable to resist Alexander's cavalry who have pushed their way onto the plain east of the river.**

2. **The Persian cavalry in the centre flee from the advancing Macedonian phalanx.**

3. **The Persian cavalry on the right wing flee from Parmenion's advancing cavalry as their left and centre crumble.**

4. **Alexander does not pursue the fleeing Persian cavalry. Instead he decides to encircle the Greek mercenaries who have not yet taken part in the battle.**

5. **Parmenion and the left wing cavalry complete the encirclement.**

6. **They ask Alexander for quarter, which is refused. The Macedonian phalanx attacks from the front. The mercenaries are further attacked from the side and rear by the Macedonian cavalry and are destroyed. The captured are enslaved.**

PHASE II – THE INFANTRY ENGAGEMENT

Late May 334 BC, attack of Alexander the Great's Macedonian and Greek allies across the River Granicus. Following the battle in the river and eastern bank, the Persian cavalry are forced back to fight on the plain. The Persian cavalry flee the battlefield, abandoning their Greek mercenaries.

XX

PARMENION

RIVER GRANICUS

Note: Gridlines are shown at intervals of 500m/547yds

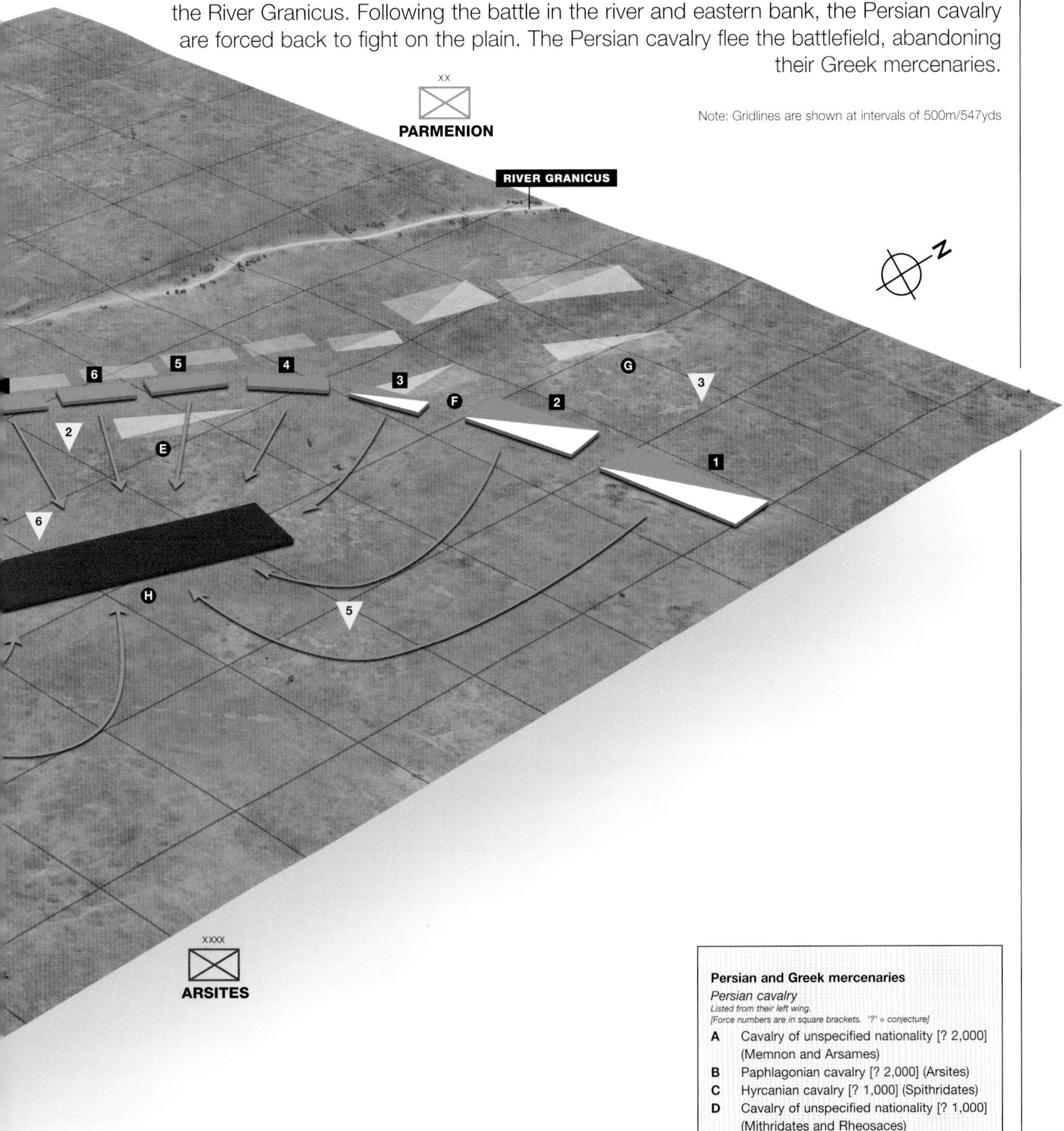

N

6 5 4 3 G 3

2 F 2

E 1

6

H 5

XXXX

ARSITES

Persian and Greek mercenaries

Persian cavalry
Listed from their left wing.
[Force numbers are in square brackets. '?' = conjecture]

A	Cavalry of unspecified nationality [? 2,000] (Memnon and Arsames)
B	Paphlagonian cavalry [? 2,000] (Arsites)
C	Hyrcanian cavalry [? 1,000] (Spithridates)
D	Cavalry of unspecified nationality [? 1,000] (Mithridates and Rheosaces)
E	Bactrian cavalry [2,000] (no known commander)
F	Cavalry of unspecified nationality [2,000] (Rheomithres)
G	Median cavalry [1,000] (no known commander)

Greek mercenaries
Behind Persian cavalry

| H | Greek mercenaries (Omares) |

This sculptural relief from Ephesus depicts some elements of Hellenistic period armour. A sword hilt in scabbard (with the scabbard's belt) at top left, plumed helmet with cheek pieces and two 'muscled' greaves to protect the shin of the lower leg. (Jona Lendering, www.livius.org)

have been able to omit a story which was of such significance and was known to have happened. That Alexander's life was very nearly lost at the battle of the Granicus, at the very outset of his career, is perhaps the most intriguing aspect of the battle.

While Alexander and the Companion cavalry were struggling to overcome the Persians on the Macedonian right wing, the phalanx in the centre was also moving forwards across the river. While they may have been showered with javelins from Persian cavalry stationed on the far bank, their progress although slow was inexorable. Plutarch (*Alex.* 16.6) states that the infantry forces of both sides engaged at this point but this claim should be disregarded as formulaic of a standard battle description where infantry in the centre of both sides typically engaged. As we have seen, at the Granicus, the Persians adopted the unusual positioning of the infantry behind the cavalry which had been marshalled along the length of the eastern river-bank. In fact, Plutarch immediately follows his statement about an infantry battle by stating that the enemy did not fight vigorously or resist for long and fled in rout *except* the Greek mercenaries who were occupying a slight rise beyond the river. As the sources do not anywhere explicitly mention Persian infantry and there is no necessary reason to postulate that there were any at the battle of the Granicus, it is better to suppose that the only infantry present were the Greek mercenaries (Hamilton, 41, Devine [1986], 270–2). As it would not have been possible for the Persian cavalry to stop the Macedonian phalanx, they would have resorted to harassing the slowly moving force by missile fire as long as practicable and then turned away.

One can only speculate as to whether the Greek mercenaries were intended to move forwards in order to engage the Macedonian phalanx as it emerged from the riverbed. Arrian (1.16.2) states that they did not move because they were 'stunned', presumably at the course of events. Meeting the Macedonians as they attempted to emerge up the riverbank would have given the hoplites some advantage over the *sarissa*-wielding phalangites, but if the cavalry on the wings collapsed, as indeed was happening, they would have been dangerously liable to a swift encirclement from the Macedonian and allied cavalry on either wing. Nevertheless, this was to be their ultimate fate despite being positioned back beyond the river line.

Diodorus (17.19.6) provides the first of only two passages in the ancient sources which describe the action which occurred on the left wing of the Macedonian line when he says that they 'gallantly met the attack of the troops posted opposite them.' This comment is not very illuminating and seems to imply that the Persians attacked with their right wing, rather than defend the river bank from which they held some defensive advantage. The Thessalian and other cavalry of the left wing under Parmenion would later play a holding role in Alexander's battles against the Persians at Issus and Gaugamela, and may have performed a similar function at the Granicus but it is hazardous to read too much into Diodorus' brief comment.

In a later passage, Diodorus (17.21.4) states that 'the Thessalian cavalry won a great reputation for valour because of the skilful handling of their squadrons and their unmatched fighting quality'. Once again, the passage is not really enlightening and, unfortunately, this is all we hear of the Macedonian left wing in the ancient sources. At some point during the battle, the Persian cavalry on their right fled, probably following the cavalry who had fled from the centre, and Parmenion's cavalry on the left wing were able to cross the river and join in the encirclement of the ill-fated Greek mercenaries whom the Persians had left behind.

On the right wing, Alexander and the Companion cavalry were gradually overcoming the Persian cavalry. They were ably assisted by the light-armed Agrianian javelinmen who were intermingled with the cavalry of both sides. Furthermore, a great number of the commanding satraps had now been slain in the attempt to kill Alexander and this must have affected both the morale and unit cohesion of the Persian cavalry. The Persian counter-attack against Amyntas' initial advance force had been continually reinforced by the Persians when they noted Alexander's entrance into the fray. Mithridates' cavalry, arriving in wedge formation, is an instance of this, although he himself was killed by Alexander (Arr. 1.15.7). This somewhat desperate attack is the only tactical movement on the Persian side mentioned in the ancient sources and may betray the inability of their command structure to cope with the failure of their original plan of killing the king. Apparently, these commanders did not appreciate the traditional military maxim that a battle plan rarely survives first contact with the enemy, and they were unable to adjust or react sufficiently to 'conditions on the ground'. The Persians now found themselves disorganized and in disarray, unable to compete with the Macedonian cavalry lance, Macedonian unit cohesion, strength, determination, and, ultimately, the Macedonian king, Alexander.

Although no precise time references are provided in the ancient sources, the two sides had perhaps been engaged for less than an hour when the pressure finally told on the Persians. Arrian (1.16.1–2) states the Persians first began to falter where Alexander was leading and he immediately follows this by saying that when the centre had given way both wings took flight. Diodorus (17.21.4) also states that 'those facing Alexander were put to flight first, and then the others.' The thrust of Alexander's charge to the immediate right of the point attacked by the advance force seems to have been where the Persian defence was initially buckled and cracked. Then, and perhaps almost simultaneously, it appears that the Persian line to the right of this point became disordered and very quickly gave way all along the line to the centre where those cavalry who had tentatively opposed the phalanx were now fleeing. Those cavalry which had committed themselves to fighting in the river and riverbed itself were dead or dying, while those on the banks were failing in their struggle to contain the push of the Companion cavalry up and onto the plain beyond. At this point a general collapse rippled out to both the far left and right wings of the Persian cavalry and, turning away from the river, they joined their comrades in fleeing the field.

The encirclement of the Greek mercenaries
The Macedonians did not pursue the Persian cavalry but instead turned their attention to the Greek mercenaries remaining on the field. By now the Macedonian phalanx had crossed the river and was moving across the roughly half mile which separated them from the mercenaries on the gently sloping plain to the east. On the left, Parmenion with the

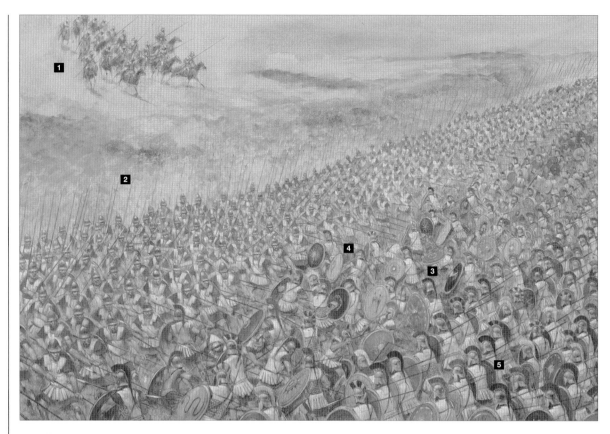

DESTRUCTION OF THE GREEK MERCENARIES AFTER THEY HAD BEEN SURROUNDED (pages 74–75)

After the Persian cavalry had been routed at the river line and fled the battlefield, the 5,000 Greek mercenaries in their hire were left holding a very slight 'rise' east of the river. They had hitherto taken no part in the battle and one ancient source says that they had remained there more 'from amazement at the unexpected result of the struggle than from any steady resolution' (Arr. 1.16.2). The Macedonian phalanx had now moved out over the eastern bank of the river, their progress practically unimpeded by the Persian cavalry in the centre before the latter's flight. The mercenaries were also now being surrounded by the Macedonian cavalry on both the left and right, as Alexander decided against pursuing the routed Persians. In this scene, remnants of the cavalry from the left wing [1] strive to join the cavalry under Parmenion which have already moved against the left and rear of the Greek phalanx.

Realising the difficulty of their predicament, the mercenaries sought surrender terms from Alexander. These were refused by the king who was 'influenced more by anger than by reason', according to the ancient historian Plutarch (*Alex.*, 16.14). Instead a furious assault was begun as the Macedonian phalanx attacked the front of the mercenary phalanx while the cavalry completed their encirclement.

The Macedonian phalanx closed ranks for attack and, marshalled to a depth of eight ranks, they presented a formidable front of *sarissae* spear points to their enemy [2]. The Macedonian *sarissa* at roughly 5–6m (c. 15-18ft) in length (effectively a long pike) significantly outreached the traditional hoplite spear at 2.5–3m (c. 7–8ft) in length, a devastating

advantage for the Macedonian infantry. The long *sarissa* enabled them to engage the first ranks of the mercenary phalanx before being immediately threatened with contact themselves and very few of the Greek hoplites would have been able to penetrate the wall of *sarissae* points before falling victim to them [3].

None the less, the Greek hoplite, heavily armed with greaves, breastplate, shield (the *hoplon* or *aspis*), helmet, thrusting spear, and short sword, was defensively formidable and marshalled at even eight ranks was difficult to dislodge. If a hoplite could manage to pierce the Macedonian line he could cause damage through overarm or underarm thrusts of his spear [4]. The mercenary phalanx also presented a problematic obstacle to cavalry as horses will not charge a fixed row of spear points. The fighting in this final phase of the battle was tough going and the Macedonian infantry probably took most, if not all, of their casualties here. It was said that Alexander even had his horse killed from underneath him after it was struck through the ribs by a sword (Plut. *Alex.* 16.7).

Ultimately, the mercenary resistance was in vain as they were gradually but remorselessly destroyed as a fighting unit. In the end, the Greek mercenaries lost over half their total force strength, and Arrian (1.16.2) says that the 2,000 who managed to survive were sent back to Macedonia in chains to work as forced labour. In this scene, the diversity of uniform and shield devices indicate the multifarious origins of the mercenaries, many of whom may have hailed from Athens, Thebes, Thessaly, the Peloponnese, as well as the Greek cities of western Asia Minor [5]. In any event, those fortunate enough to survive were unlikely ever to see their homelands again.

Thessalian and allied horse began to encircle the right side of the 5,000 mercenaries while, on the right, Alexander and the Companion cavalry were doing the same.

Abandoned by the Persian cavalry, the heavily armed Greek hoplites were in no position to escape the Macedonian cavalry. In this desperate position they asked Alexander for quarter (Plut. *Alex.* 16.13). Despite the apparent hopelessness of their situation, the mercenaries probably thought this petition stood a good chance of success. Although clearly outnumbered, the body of mercenaries remained a formidable fighting force which would be costly for Alexander to reduce. They perhaps thought that Alexander would be happy to spare his men this unnecessary combat and simply take them on into his army. This calculation, even if forced by their position, was not irrational. However, neither they nor probably even the Macedonians themselves understood Alexander's mind at the culmination of this his first battle against the Persian Empire.

Plutarch (*Alex.* 16.14) says that Alexander 'influenced more by anger than by reason' refused the mercenaries' appeal for terms and straightaway led the final attack. Perhaps influenced by a desire to make a point to Greek mercenaries in Persian pay or simply carried away by the fury of the action and his own near fatal experience in the river, Alexander was not in any mood to accept terms. The latter is certainly how Plutarch portrays the event. However, it may very well have been the case that Alexander's intentions were not entirely unthinking. Theoretically, these Greek mercenaries were in violation of their obligation to fight against the Persians as agreed by the Greek states at Corinth in 337 BC (cf. Arr. 1.16.6). Alexander, like his father Philip before him, was officially leader (*hegemon*) of the allied Greek and Macedonians in this expedition of vengeance and liberation against Persia, and Alexander may have wished to send a clear message to recalcitrant or reluctant Greeks that those who accepted Persian gold were treasonous to this enterprise and would not be spared.

The Macedonians now attacked the Greek mercenaries *en masse*. Surrounded by the cavalry, they were attacked from the front by the phalanx (Arr. 1.16.2). Few details of this phase of the battle are provided

Casualty figures for the battle of the Granicus

	Arrian,1.16.4	Diodorus, 17.21.6	Justin, 11.6.11--12	Plutarch, 16.7
Macedonian				
Cavalry	'about' 25 Companions 'over' 60 other cavalry		120	25 (citing Aristobulus)
Infantry	'about' 30		9	9 (citing Aristobulus)
Persian				
Cavalry	'only about' 1,000	'more than' 2,000		2,500
Greek mercenaries	'none escaped' except the captured 'about' 2,000 captured	'more than' 10,000 'upwards of' 20,000 captured		20,000

Table of casualties as related by the ancient sources.

in the ancient sources, but the mercenaries may have formed a sort of 'pike square' to counter the encirclement. Outnumbered, the experienced and disciplined mercenaries fought fiercely after their failed parley left them with no other choice. The combat was heavy going for the Macedonians and, according to Plutarch (*Alex.* 16.7), it was in this phase of the battle where they suffered the greatest number of casualties. It was said that Alexander even had his horse killed from underneath him after it was struck through the ribs by a sword (Plut. *Alex.* 16.7). Nevertheless, the final outcome was never in doubt. Arrian (1.16.2) reports that the mercenaries were 'cut up' in the attack and that 'none of them escaped except such as might have concealed themselves among the dead.' About 2,000 mercenaries were ultimately captured and these were led away in chains, intended for slave labour back in Macedon.

Whether this bloody denouement sated Alexander's anger on the day is not recorded, but the perhaps unnecessary attack was costly for the king. In fact, he mitigated this hard-line approach to Greek mercenaries in future encounters, often taking those who surrendered into his service. However, that policy shift could not undo the memory of his treatment of the mercenaries at the Granicus and in general Greek mercenaries in Persian pay felt they had better fight to the death rather than risk asking for terms from Alexander.

Casualties

Persian cavalry losses at the battle were moderated by the fact that their flight from the battlefield was not pursued by Alexander's cavalry. Arrian (1.16.4) says that 'only about' 1,000 cavalry were killed before the rout, while Diodorus (17.21.6) claims that 'not less than' 2,000 cavalry perished. Plutarch (*Alex.* 16.7) provides the highest figure when he states that 2,500 cavalry were killed. If the total Persian cavalry figure at the battle was slightly more than 10,000, as is maintained in this book, then the Persian cavalry suffered losses of around 10–20 per cent. This is not an unusually high ratio for the losing side in ancient warfare.

However, the percentage of commanders killed was much higher and Diodorus (17.21.4) implies that this was a significant cause of the Persian collapse. Arrian (1.16.3) lists the fallen Persian commanders as 'Niphates, Petines, Spithridates, viceroy of Lydia, Mithrobuzanes, governor of Cappadocia, Mithridates, the son-in-law of Darius, Arbupales, son of Darius the son of Artaxerxes, Pharnaces, brother of the wife of Darius, and Omares, commander of the mercenaries.' Moreover, it is likely that Rhoesaces was killed in the combat with Alexander, which would mean that nine of 14, or virtually two-thirds, of the named Persian commanders at the battle, perished.

It was the Greek mercenaries who bore the brunt of the casualties on the losing side. As it has been argued in this book that the number of mercenaries present was considerably lower than the figures provided in sources, we can dismiss the inflated and exaggerated claims of 'more than 10,000' and '20,000' infantry killed, provided by Diodorus (17.21.6) and Plutarch (*Alex.* 16.7) respectively. Arrian says that about 2,000 of the mercenaries were eventually captured which would entail that 2,000 to 3,000 of the Greek mercenaries were killed or seriously wounded in the final phase of the battle. Of course, this very high ratio of 50 to 60 per cent is explained by their encirclement and Alexander's

A gold model chariot from the Oxus treasure, Achaemenid Persian, from the region of Takht-i-Kuwad, Tadjikistan, 5–4th century BC. This remarkable model is one of the most outstanding pieces in the Oxus treasure, which dates mainly from the 5th–4th century BC. The Oxus treasure is the most important surviving collection of gold and silver to have survived from the Achaemenid period. The model chariot is pulled by four horses or ponies. In it are two figures wearing Median dress. The Medes were from Iran, the centre of the Achaemenid empire. The front of the chariot is decorated with the Egyptian dwarf-god Bes, a popular protective deity. (The British Museum/HIP/Topfoto)

fury but it is shocking to contemplate the butchery required to reach such percentages, even based on a minimalist force figure of 5,000. The carnage was clearly terrible.

On the Macedonian side the casualties were far fewer. Roughly 25 Companion cavalry were lost from Socrates' *ile* in the initial attack and, according to Arrian (1.16.4) 60 'other' cavalry were lost as well. The 'other' cavalry are not specified but many probably came from the *prodromoi* and Paeonians who accompanied Socrates' *ile* in the vanguard and met the difficult initial Persian resistance in the river. Some of these may also have come from the Thessalian and allied cavalry with Parmenion on the left wing as well. Plutarch (*Alex.* 16.7), citing Aristobulus as his source, says that 25 cavalry perished (likely the 25 Companion referred to in Arrian, whose source was Ptolemy), while Justin (11.6.11) claims 120 cavalry perished.

Even lower figures are provided for the Macedonian infantry. Both Plutarch (*Alex.* 16.7) and Justin (11.6.11) claim that only nine Macedonian infantry fell in the battle, while Arrian (1.16.4) says that 'about' 30 died. These figures might seem unbelievably low, perhaps the result of propaganda to minimize Macedonian dead and highlight Persian loses. It has been argued, however, (Hammond [1989]) that there are good reasons to believe that these figures are generally accurate, and it should be recalled that the infantry phalanx did not actually engage the enemy until they met the surrounded Greek mercenaries on the plain beyond the river. Here the lethality of the *sarissa* against a trapped enemy would have been particularly fatal. It is also important to note that these figures from the sources relate only the dead and not the wounded, which would have increased the total number of casualties.

Alexander made a point of visiting the wounded after the battle, and the following day he buried with much ceremony the Macedonian fallen, as well as the Persian commanders and Greek mercenaries who had perished (Arr. 1.16.6, Diod 17.21.4, Justin 11.6.12). The greatest tribute was reserved for the 25 fallen Companions when Alexander commissioned his personal court sculptor, Lysippus, to erect bronze statues in their honour at Dium in Macedon where they remained until removed to Rome by Quintus Metellus Macedonicus in 146 BC. For the parents and children of the dead left behind in Macedon, Alexander remitted taxes and relieved them of certain services due to the state (Arr. 1.16.5, Justin 11.6.12). In addition, he sent 300 captured Persian panoplies to Athens to be hung up on the Acropolis as a votive offering to Athena. With these trophies was inscribed: 'Alexander, son of Philip, and the Greeks, except the Spartans, [donate these spoils] from the barbarians who live in Asia.' (Arr. 1.16.7, Plut. *Alex.* 16.8). With these gestures, Alexander proclaimed the importance of his victory at the River Granicus throughout Greece, Macedonia, and Asia Minor.

AFTERMATH

THE MARCH SOUTH TO THE COAST

After the battle, Alexander made Calas satrap of the now conquered Hellespontine Phrygia. Arsites, the previous satrap, fled to the interior of Greater Phrygia where he committed suicide, perhaps unable to face the Great King after the defeat. The city of Zeleia from where the satraps had set out to the River Granicus was pardoned because Alexander decided that they had been compelled to succour the Persians. Parmenion was sent farther east to secure the provincial capital of Dascylium which he found abandoned by the Persian military (Arr. 1.17.1–2).

Alexander and the army headed south to the city of Sardis and, about ten miles outside of the city, he was met by Mithrenes, the garrison commander, who surrendered to him the very defensible citadel and the significant treasury without a fight. Four days later, travelling south-west towards the coast, Alexander reached Ephesus where the Persian garrison and their mercenaries had abandoned the city prior to his arrival. The cities of Lydia went over to Alexander without a quarrel, but farther south in Caria he was to meet resistance.

At the coastal city of Miletus, Alexander was forced to commence his first siege of the campaign. Fortunately, the Greek fleet reached the area three days before the arrival of the Persian fleet from the south. In a

**The Hellenistic theatre and other remains from ancient Ephesus.
(Jona Lendering, www.livius.org)**

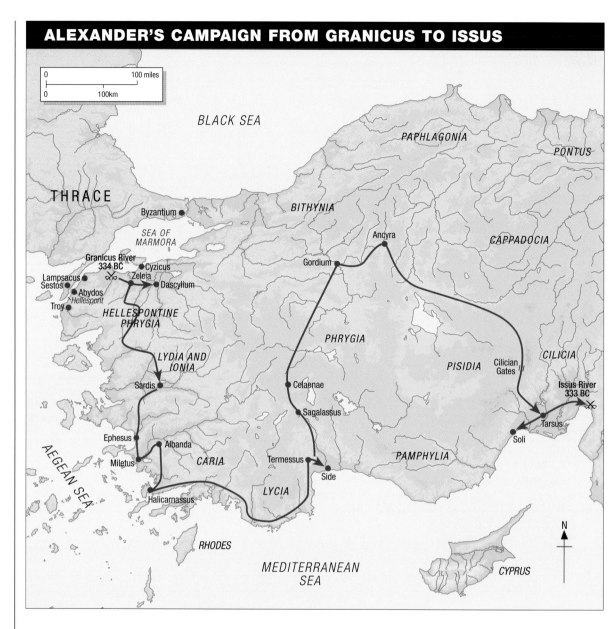

combined sea and land operation, Alexander was finally able to capture the city and the Persian navy, unable to assist in the defence, retired. Alexander now decided to disband the bulk of his navy due to its cost, and instead capture the cities and ports on the coast from which the Persian navy might operate.

THE SIEGE OF HALICARNASSUS

The most important of these cities in the vicinity was Halicarnassus which, set in a natural amphitheatre, was well fortified with a number of strong citadels. Moreover, Memnon of Rhodes, now given full command of the west by Darius, had gathered the Greek mercenaries of the nearby cities to defend the fortress and, without the possibility of a naval

blockade by Alexander, the city could be indefinitely supplied by sea. Initial Macedonian attempts to take the city were costly and fruitless, and, on one occasion, the one and only time in Alexander's career, he was forced to ask for a truce to recover his dead. Despite effective counter attacks and the construction of curtain walls to defend breaches created by the siege engines, Memnon and his commanders realized they could not ultimately withstand the siege. They burned the city and outer fortifications and withdrew to the inner citadels. Deciding it would be too costly to storm these fortifications, Alexander left a holding force under Ptolemy and entered Lycia to the east.

The theatre at Miletus.
Note that the fortifications
overlooking the theatre
are from the Byzantine period.
(Jona Lendering, www.livius.org)

Route to Gordion

Travelling through the mountainous region of Lycia he reached the coast at Phaselis. The army headed into Pamphylia via a specially constructed pass over Mt Climax while Alexander and a smaller group passed along the coast. At one point the coastal road was submerged beneath a sea driven by southern winds. In what was later interpreted as a sign of divine favour, the wind suddenly changed and, as the sea receded, Alexander was able to pass. After bivouacking in Aspendus, he campaigned against the rugged mountain towns of Pisidia before reaching Caelenae on the road to Gordion in the satrapy of Greater Phrygia. Reaching the city a few weeks later, Alexander probably met up with Parmenion and the Greek allies who had previously been sent to campaign against remnants of Persian forces on the Anatolian plateau (Bosworth [1993], 49, 51).

In Gordion, Alexander was shown the intricate knot which bound the yoke and shaft of the legendary king Gordias' ox-cart. The local inhabitants held that whoever should untie the knot would become king of Asia, a challenge Alexander could not resist. According to Plutarch, Alexander became frustrated at his inability to loosen the knot and resorted to hacking it free with his sword. However, another account attributed to Aristobulus says that Alexander merely pulled out the pin joining the yoke and shaft to reveal the loose ends which he then unravelled (Plut. *Alex.* 18.1–2, cf. Arr. 2.3). In any event, his blushes were spared and the oracular prophecy appeared to be fulfilled.

The route to Issus

During his stay at Gordion in the summer of 333 BC, Alexander must have received the unwelcome intelligence that Memnon, formerly holed up in Halicarnassus, was now freely operating against the islands of the western Aegean. These actions endangered his supply and communications to Macedon and threatened to undo the work of the previous year's

Sculptural relief of a 'yuana' from Persepolis. The Persians called the Greeks 'yuana' because their contact was chiefly with the 'Ionian' Greeks who settled had the western coast of Asia Minor. (Jona Lendering, www.livius.org)

campaigning. However, in one of the most fortuitous events of Alexander's career, this potentially serious menace was removed when Memnon died of an illness during the siege of Mytilene. Furthermore, it appears that Darius then had a change of heart about carrying on operations behind Alexander's march and ordered his fleet, and the mercenaries operating with them, to return east with the intention of joining the army he was already collecting from all areas of the empire.

Alexander now marched his army south through Ancyra towards the Cilician Gates which passed through the Taurus mountain range and into the fertile Aleian plain at the north-west corner of the Mediterranean. Forcing the Cilician Gates with relative ease, he raced to the city of Tarsus in one day, capturing the city before it could be burned. While Alexander was taken ill after swimming in the freezing waters of the River Cydnus near Tarsus, Darius led his vast native army, swelled by 30,000 Greek mercenaries, from Babylon to Sochi near the Amanus range east of the River Issus. After recovering from his illness, Alexander set out to find Darius and, after much searching and complicated manoeuvrings, the two armies finally met on the plain through which the river emptied into the Gulf of Issus. At last Alexander was to face the Great King directly on the field of battle.

THE BATTLEFIELD TODAY

As it did in antiquity, the ancient Granicus (the modern Biga Çay) flows from the mountains of north-western Anatolia and empties into the Sea of Marmara. To access the site a car is required which may be hired in Istanbul. At least two days are required as the drive from Istanbul to the site will take from seven to eight hours. It is recommended that the traveller stay the night in Çanakkale and perhaps allow an extra day or two to take in the archaeological site of ancient Troy and the First World War Gallipoli battlefields, both of which are near Çanakkale.

From Istanbul follow the D100 motorway west through Silvri to the D110 through the city of Tekirdag to Kesan where you should take the D550 south down to the Gallipoli peninsula. The quickest route would be to cross at Gelibolu, approximately five hours' drive from Istanbul, where there are ferries to Lapeski (ancient Lampsacus). From Lapeski follow the D200 motorway along the Marmara coast to the town of Biga from where the battlefield lies slightly north of the town.

The Turkish authorities have placed this road sign to indicate the way to the 'Granicus Battlefield'. However, the battle occurred some two miles south, further upstream the river.

The confluence of the the Biga Çay and the Koca Çay which formed the extreme right extent of the battlefield as viewed from the western (Macedonian) bank.

Alternatively, you can follow the D550 farther south to Eceabat where the ferries run frequently across the Dardanelles to the lovely town of Çanakkale. Here pleasant accommodation and waterside restaurants may be found. From Çanakkale follow the E-90 road north through Lapeski along the D200 motorway to Biga. Roughly five miles before the town of Biga there is a sign-posted turn-off to the little town of Karabiga, the ancient settlement of Priapus, on the coast of Marmara. The drive from Çanakkale to the Granicus takes less than two hours and largely follows the route Alexander would have taken via Percote and Lampsacus (Lapeski), although he may have travelled inland in the vicinity of the town of Balikiçe°me, via the ancient but yet unidentified towns of Colonae and Hermotus, approaching the river Granicus in the low valley formed by the Kocaba° Çay.

The rather straight road to Karabiga passes through the heavily cultivated land of the 'Granicus' plain and roughly two miles before the town of Karabiga the authorities have placed a brown sign at a right turning which reads 'Granikos: Sava° Alani' ('Granicus Battlefield'). The dirt track indicated by the sign crosses a wide modern irrigation canal and roughly one mile later terminates at a rough stone ford not suitable for normal cars. This is the River Granicus which even in May/June is, at this point, wide (*c.* 50 feet) and free-flowing, if somewhat shallow. The mouth of the river can be seen under half a mile away to the north where the Sea of Marmara opens out. Although this is the ancient Granicus, the actual site of the battle did not occur here but rather farther upstream roughly two miles south of the location indicated by the road sign. Nevertheless, at this point, the relatively low and treeless banks give a good indication of how the actual battlefield may have appeared in antiquity, particularly with regard to Parmenion's position on the left of the Macedonian line.

To reach the actual battlefield it is necessary to return to the main road (the track along the west bank of the river is unsuitable for normal cars after two miles) to the village of Çinarköprü five miles south. The tiny village of Çinarköprü is a short distance off the main road and leads to a bridge which crosses the Granicus just south of the confluence of

This is quite possibly the first photograph taken of the river Granicus. Taken *c.*1900 by a German army officer Oberleutenant W. von Marées. It clearly indicates that, unlike today, the banks were much lower and the vegetation sparser. The two horses in the river indicate how shallow it is in summer.

the Biga Çay and the Koca Çay which formed the extreme right extent of the battlefield as viewed from the western (Macedonian) bank. As argued in this book, the battle lines stretched from a point north of the confluence of the Biga Çay and the Koca Çay to roughly two-and-a-half miles northwards downstream. To a great extent, this corresponds to the tree-lined banks which, at ground level, indicate the existence of the river in the otherwise flat and featureless plain surrounding it. In fact, the tree line of the Granicus becomes very distinct when viewed from nearby high ground. Just over half a mile due east of the leftmost extent of the battlefield lies the village of Çesmealti at the base of the small hills which run south towards Biga. From here, or from the tiny hamlet of Adiye on the slight hills immediately south-west of the river, the tree line of the river clearly stands out immediately east of the stand of plane trees from which the village of Çinarköprü receives its name, i.e. 'Plane tree bridge'.

Although the banks of the river are now high, steep and rather heavily wooded it is possible to access the bed of the river from paths near the Çinarköprü Bridge. In May/June the river does not occupy the full width of the bed but meanders as a small stream with occasional rivulets cutting through the exposed sand and gravel riverbed upon which sporadically grows small scrub and vegetation. With the exception of steep and narrow paths which lead to the diesel pumps and hoses through which the farmers draw water for their fields out of the river, it is not possible to descend or ascend the banks along the course of the battlefield. At points the main stream appears quite deep and swift flowing, although in summer it is mainly shallow and slow moving.

What immediately strikes the modern viewer (and the author bases this account on a field walk of the site in late May 2006) is that the description of the cavalry battle in and about the river as described in the ancient sources is difficult to square with the present topographical reality. Moreover, and perhaps more worryingly, is that the present topography little resembles the accounts of visitors of 30 years ago who describe the river as mostly easily fordable and the banks accessible to cavalry at virtually all points of the battlefield (Foss, Hammond [1980],

This photo taken *c.* 1910 by Walter Leaf for his work, *Troy: A Study in Homeric Geography*, shows the plain of Adresteia looking south. The Granicus River runs in a channel just behind the two camels in the middle distance.

Nikolitsis). Photographs taken 30 years ago do resemble the somewhat indistinct photographs taken by the German army officer Oberleutenant W. von Marées who explored the area at the turn of the 20th century AD with his colleague Oberst A. Janke. In modern times they were first to have walked the battlefield and identified the river as the ancient Granicus. In his 1904 work, *Auf Alexanders des Grossen Pfaden: Eine Reise durch Kleinasian*, Janke provided a photo by von Marées (this is the earliest photo of the River 'Granicus' that the author is aware of) which indicates topography similar to that photographed by Nikolitsis (plates 2-8) and described by Foss (500–2, figs. 3–9) and Hammond (1980), (77-80). Allowing for a considerable increase in vegetation on the river banks since antiquity, it was still possible to reconstruct, given the physical topography as it was 30 years ago, a massed cavalry action in the river and along its banks. Unfortunately, this is not readily possible today.

There may be two explanations for this. It appears that the river is being partially dredged to increase its flow in summertime *and* that the banks have been gradually increased or, at least, the lower 'gaps' which breached banks of any considerable height and allowed easy access to the riverbed have been filled in with modern earthworks. A crane was seen dredging the river bed and drawing up gravel on the lower courses of the river where the banks are much lower than those at the battlefield. In addition, numerous lorries were seen on the track of the eastern bank along the river where the banks appear to be in the process of being further embanked to support the farmed fields there.

It is perhaps not surprising that the river has been altered in this way. The area surrounding the Biga Çay is very heavily cultivated and the plain itself provides some of largest and most arable tracks of farmland on the north-western coast of the Anatolian peninsula. The river, from which is drawn so much of the water used to irrigate these fields, is now, apparently, being managed to ensure a suitable supply of water for irrigation in summer. Conversely, the increased embankments protect the fields from winter floods when, as can be seen from the width of the riverbed and rubbish strewn high in the trees and vegetation on the banks, the river must become quite swollen and swift.

The monumental 'Gate of all Nations' at the Persian royal palace in Persepolis. The gate was finished by Xerxes in the second phase of building at the site (*c.* 460 BC). This view from the south-west shows two colossal 'bull-men' standing at the rear doorway. (Jona Lendering, www.livius.org)

It may even be the case that the embanking and subsequent levelling of the plain has erased the small slight rise of three metres which Janke noted (Hammond, 80 note 20) at the turn of the 20th century and which may have even been a more prominent rise before the intervening years of ploughing removed any trace of the 'hill' (*lophos*) upon which Plutarch says the shocked Greek mercenaries witnessed the cavalry battle and unsuccessfully sought surrender terms.

None the less, as seen at present, the Biga Çay is still the ancient Granicus, despite a minority view that the river has since changed course. (See Hammond [1980], 77 and Devine [1988], 4) and it is still not too difficult to image the battle while viewing the river northwards from the bridge at Çinarköprü.

Troy

The hill of Hisarlik, ancient Troy, inscribed as a UNESCO World Heritage Site in 1998, is roughly 19 miles south of Çanakkale on well signposted roads. The scene of Homer's epic poem the *Illiad*, excavations were begun in 1871 by a founder of modern archaeology, Heinrich Schliemann, and have continued intermittently to the present. The mound comprises no less than ten distinct levels built upon from the early 3rd millennium BC to the Byzantine bishopric of 1000 AD. However, the allure of Troy is the sixth level dated to the late Bronze Age and associated with the events and heroes related in the *Iliad*. An excavated stretch of wall with tower foundations from 'Troy VI' is one of the highlights of any visit to Troy. The complex site is well laid out and an excellent guidebook (revised in 2005) by the current director of excavations, Manfred Korfmann, is available at shops just outside the entrance to the site. For those interested in the ancient world, Troy should be added to the itinerary of any trip to the Granicus.

Gallipoli

The Gallipoli peninsula also contains sites for those interested in more modern military conflicts. The battlefields and cemeteries of the ill-fated

Gallipoli campaign of the First World War may be found there. In 1915, the Allied attempt to force the Dardanelles, capture Istanbul, and knock the Ottoman Turks out of the war foundered on the southern tip of the peninsula at great loss to Commonwealth and Turkish forces alike. The battlefield and cemeteries are located at two places. The first lies on the southern tip of the peninsula at Hellas Point where the mainly British landings were made. The stark obelisk of Hellas Point lists the British and Commonwealth forces who fell there, and is mirrored by the impressive Turkish Çanakkale Martyrs Memorial to the east. Roughly ten miles north of the tip of the Gallipoli peninsula lies ANZAC Cove where Australian and New Zealand forces were landed to open another front. Little headway was made in the steep and difficult terrain, as the numerous little cemeteries indicate. High on the ridges overlooking the island of Imbros lays Çonkbayiri Hill where the Turkish dead are remembered in another impressive monument. The sense of loss, conciliated by a mutual respect testified on both sides through these monuments, is a moving experience.

BIBLIOGRAPHY

Primary sources

Inexpensive editions of English translations of Arrian and Plutarch are published by Penguin books under the following titles:

Arrian, *The Campaigns of Alexander.* Trans Aubrey De Sâelincourt with a preface by J.R. Hamilton (1971)

Plutarch, *The Age of Alexander: Nine Greek lives*. Trans Ian Scott-Kilvert (1973)

Editions of Arrian, Plutarch and Diodorus in English translation with facing Greek text are available in the Loeb Classical Library series. Translations in this book are largely taken (although occasionally adapted) from these volumes and are cited in the text as follows:

Arr. = Arrian (1976 v.1, 1983 v.2). *History of Alexander and Indica*. 2 vols. Trans P.A. Brunt, Harvard University Press, Cambridge, Mass; Heinemann, London.

Diod. = Diodorus (1952 v.7, 1963 v. 8). *Library of History*, Vol. 7 trans by C. Sherman and vol. 8 trans by C. Bradford Welles, W. Heinemann, London; Harvard University Press, Cambridge, Mass.

Plut. *Alex*. = Plutarch (1919). 'Life of Alexander' in *Plutarch's Lives*. Vol. 7. Trans by B. Perrin, Heinemann, London; Harvard University Press, Cambridge, Mass.

A new translation of the ancient historian, Justin's, account of Alexander's campaigns is Justin, M.J.. *Epitome of the Philippic history of Pompeius Trogus: books 11-12, Alexander the Great*. Trans. by J. Yardley and W. Heckel, Clarendon Press, Oxford (1997)

Secondary literature

There are a great number of earlier scholarly accounts of the battle of the Granicus, mainly written by German scholars, which cover virtually all possible reconstructions of the battle. These are very usefully summarized by Nikolitsis (11–12) and analysed by Badian (1977). In addition, general histories of ancient Greece and Alexander the Great usually contain reconstructions of the battle, e.g. Peter Green's (1991), 489–512, heavily revised view of the battle. Only those works which are directly cited in the text are listed here. The standard account of Alexander's career is now Bosworth (1993).

Anson, E., 'The Persian Fleet in 334' – *Classical Philology* 84 (1), pp. 44–49 (1989)

Austin, M. M., 'Alexander and the Macedonian invasion of Asia: Aspects of the historiography of war and empire in antiquity', *War and Society in the Greek World*, Rich, J. and Shipley, G., Routledge, London and New York, pp.197–223 (1993)

Badian, E., 'The Battle of the Granicus: A New Look' in *Ancient Macedonia* Thessaloniki, Institute for Balkan Studies, 2, pp.271–93 (1977)

Badian, E., 'Darius III', *Harvard Studies in Classical Philology* 100, pp.241–67 (2000)

Bosworth, A.B. *A Historical Commentary on Arrian's History of Alexander*, Clarendon Press, Oxford (1980)

Bosworth, A.B., *Conquest and Empire: the Reign of Alexander the Great*, Cambridge University Press, Cambridge (1993)

Briant, P., *From Cyrus to Alexander: a history of the Persian Empire*, Eisenbraun, Winona Lake IN (2002)

Brunt, P. A., 'Alexander's Macedonian Cavalry', *Journal of Hellenic Studies* 83, pp. 27–46 (1963)

Davis, E.W., 'The Persian Battle Plan at the Granicus', in *The James Sprunt Studies in History and Political Science*, Chapel Hill, NC. 46, pp.34–44 (1964)

Devine, A.M., 'Demythologizing the Battle of the Granicus', *Phoenix - the Journal of the Classical Association of Canada* 40 (3), pp.265–78 (1986)

Devine, A.M., 'A Pawn-Sacrifice at the Battle of the Granicus, the Origins of a Favorite Strategem of Alexander-the-Great', in *Ancient World* 18 (1–2), pp.3–20 (1988)

Engels, D.W., *Alexander the Great and the Logistics of the Macedonian Army*, University of California Press, Berkeley, London (1978)

Errington, R.M., *A History of Macedonia*, Berkeley and Los Angeles (1990)

Foss, C., 'The Battle of the Granicus: A New Look', in *Ancient Macedonia*, 2, pp.495–502, Institute for Balkan Studies, Thessaloniki (1977)

Gaebel, R.E., *Cavalry Operations in the Ancient Greek World*, University of Oklahoma Press, Norman (2002)

Garvin, E.E., Darius III and Homeland Defense, *Crossroads of history: the Age of Alexander*, W. Heckel and L. A. Tritle, Regina Books, Claremont, Calif., pp.87–111 (2003) Berkel

Green, P., *Alexander of Macedon, 356-323 B.C.: a historical biography.*, University of California Press, Berkley; Oxford (1991)

Hamilton, J.R., *Plutarch: Alexander a commentary*, Clarendon Press, Oxford (1969)

Hammond, N.G. L., 'The Battle of the Granicus River', in *Journal of Hellenic Studies* 100, pp.73–88 (1980)

Hammond, N.G.L., 'Casualties and Reinforcements of Citizen Soldiers in Greece and Macedonia', in *Journal of Hellenic Studies* 109, pp.56–68 (1989)

Harl, K., Alexander's Cavalry Battle at the Granicus, in *Polis and Polemos: Essays on Politics, War and History in Honor of Donald Kagan*, Hamilton, C.D. and Krentz, P., Regina Books, Claremont, Calif., pp.303–26 (1997)

Heckel, W., *The Marshals of Alexander's Empire.*, Routledge, London (1992)

Heckel, W. and R Jones, *Macedonian Warrior: Alexander's elite infantryman*, Osprey, Oxford (2006)

Kent, R.G., *Old Persian: grammar, texts, lexicon*, American Oriental Society, New Haven, Conn. (1953)

Lane Fox, R., *Alexander the Great.*, Allen Lane, London (1973)

Manti, P.A., 'The Cavalry Sarissa', in *Ancient World* 8, pp.73–80 (1983)

Markle, M.M., III. 'The Macedonian Sarissa, Spear, and Related Armor', in *American Journal of Archaeology* 81 (3), pp.323–39 (1977)

Markle, M.M., 'Use of the Sarissa by Philip and Alexander of Macedon', in *American Journal of Archaeology* 82 (4), pp.483–97 (1978)

McCoy, W.J.. 'Memnon of Rhodes at the Granicus', *American Journal of Philology* 110 (3), pp.413–33 (1989)

Milns, R. D., 'Alexander's Macedonian Cavalry and Diodorus 17.17.4', in *Journal of Hellenic Studies* 86, pp.167–68 (1966)

Nikolitsis, N.T.. *The Battle of the Granicus*, , Svenska Institutet i Athen, Stockholm and Lund (1974)

Rahe, P.A., 'The Military Situation in Western Asia on the Eve of Cunaxa', in *American Journal of Philology* 101, pp.79–98 (1980)

Rahe, P.A.. 'The Annihilation of the Sacred Band at Chaeronea', in *American Journal of Archaeology* 85, pp.84–87 (1981)

Ruzicka, S., 'A Note on Philip's Persian War', in *American Journal of Ancient History* 10, pp.84–91 (1985)

Sekunda, N., *The Persian army, 560–330 BC*, Osprey, Oxford (1992)

Other resources

For those interested in the battle of the Granicus and Alexander the Great outside of printed media there are numerous resources available on the internet. These can be accessed via a search engine and simple word search. However, as is always true of any internet search, the quality and accuracy of the sites is highly variable. In this case, critical judgement is especially required.

Two feature-length movies have been produced about the life of Alexander. *Alexander the Great* (1956) starring Sir Richard Burton does portray the battle of the Granicus, including the incident where Alexander's life is saved by 'Black' Cleitus. The indifferently received *Alexander* (2004) by Oliver Stone only mentions the battle, which is not depicted, although somewhat strangely the event where Cleitus dramatically saves Alexander's life at the Granicus is conflated into the battle of Gaugamela. Unfortunately, the excellent television programme by Michael Wood, *In the Footsteps of Alexander the Great* (BBC 2005) does not cover the Granicus but is a first-rate survey of Alexander's life.

INDEX